北京大学研究生学术规范与创新能力建设丛书

生命科学论文写作指南

BIOMEDICAL WRITING FOR YOUNG INVESTIGATORS
WHOSE FIRST LANGUAGE IS CHINESE

〔加拿大〕白青云（Iain C. Bruce） 著

图书在版编目(CIP)数据

生命科学论文写作指南/(加拿大)白青云(Bruce,I.)著. —北京:北京大学出版社,2012.1
(北京大学研究生学术规范与创新能力建设丛书)
ISBN 978-7-301-19892-6

Ⅰ.①生… Ⅱ.①白… Ⅲ.①生命科学-英语-论文-写作 Ⅳ.①H315

中国版本图书馆 CIP 数据核字(2011)第 256564 号

书　　　名：生命科学论文写作指南
著作责任者：〔加拿大〕白青云　著
丛 书 主 持：周志刚
责 任 编 辑：泮颖雯
标 准 书 号：ISBN 978-7-301-19892-6/G·3280
出 版 发 行：北京大学出版社
地　　　址：北京市海淀区成府路 205 号　100871
网　　　址：http://www.jycb.org　http://www.pup.cn
电 子 邮 箱：zyl@pup.pku.edu.cn
电　　　话：邮购部 62752015　发行部 62750672　编辑部 62767346
　　　　　　出版部 62754962
印 刷 者：北京汇林印务有限公司
经 销 者：新华书店
　　　　　　730 毫米×980 毫米　16 开本　11.5 印张　160 千字
　　　　　　2012 年 1 月第 1 版　2013 年 4 月第 2 次印刷
定　　　价：25.00 元

未经许可,不得以任何方式复制或抄袭本书之部分或全部内容。
版权所有,侵权必究
举报电话：010-62752024　电子邮箱：fd@pup.pku.edu.cn

北京大学研究生学术规范与创新能力建设丛书

学术委员会
主　　任：许智宏
副主任：林建华　柯　杨　张国有
委　　员：甘子钊　杨芙清　袁行霈　厉以宁
　　　　　方伟岗　文　兰　昌增益　陈尔强
　　　　　陶　澍　朱苏力　王缉思　陈学飞
　　　　　温儒敏　牛大勇　叶　朗　王明舟
　　　　　王仰麟

编辑委员会
主　　任：林建华
副主任：王　宪　王仰麟　张黎明
委　　员：高　岱　生玉海　段丽萍
　　　　　郑兰哲　贾爱英

丛书策划：北京大学研究生院　北京大学出版社

本书编委会

主任：白青云　浙江大学医学院教授

委员：（按姓名拼音顺序排列）

　　丁跃民　浙江大学城市学院讲师

　　贾爱英　北京大学研究生院研究员

　　姜　怡　北京大学分子医学研究所助理研究员

　　刘　健　北京大学分子医学研究所助理研究员

　　罗建红　浙江大学医学院教授

　　夏　强　浙江大学医学院教授

　　余　方　浙江大学医学院副教授

　　余　海　浙江大学医学院教授

　　周　专　北京大学分子医学研究所教授

丛 书 总 序

21世纪的竞争,归根结底是人才的竞争。党的十七大明确提出要优先发展教育,提高高等教育质量,建设人力资源强国。高等教育担负着为国家培养高素质创新人才、为社会提供一流服务的重任,大力发展高等教育是实现我国由教育大国向教育强国转变的战略手段,北京大学正努力地朝着建设世界一流的研究型大学的目标迈进。

近十年,国家启动两期"985工程"和"211工程",加快推进了我国高等教育的改革和发展。现在,"985工程"和"211工程"三期也已经或即将启动,这必将继续推动我国高等教育的进步,促进教育质量的提高、学科设置的改善、学校管理的改革和人才队伍的建设。在此期间,中国高等教育积极开拓国际视野,增强与国外大学特别是世界知名大学的交流与合作,通过联合培养、交换学习等方式让教师和学生接触国际学术前沿,并通过引进海外优秀人才、教学互访等方式加强了与国外大学的合作,吸纳了很多先进的教学方法与科技成果。

世界各国特别是发达国家,长期以来都把培养拔尖创新人才作为国家发展战略,并作为增强其国家核心竞争力的重要手段。从一定意义上说,研究生教育代表着一个国家高等教育的水平,研究生培养直接关系创新型国家建设目标的实现。研究生教育的任务就在于培养出国家人力资源金字塔中的顶尖人才,这也决定了研究生教育具有精英性、专业性和创新性的特征。研究生教育的培养质量代表着中国科学研究的能力和潜力,引领着中国科技和文化的发展方向,是建设社会主义和谐社会的重要力量。随着全球化的不断深入和扩大,如何把我国从一个高等教育大国建设成为高等教育强国是我们面临的重要挑战,如何进一步提高研究生培养质量也成为我们亟待解决的问题。

受历史条件、客观因素的制约,目前我国的研究生教育存在一些阻碍其长足发展的瓶颈区域。研究生培养质量有待提高,导师制度有待健全,学术道德观念亟需加强,自主创新的能力和水平也应不断提高。这些问题提醒我们高校教育工作者,要结合我国教育实际和客观条件,进行积极有效地培养机制改革,提高教师和学生从事科学研究的积极性和能力,加强学术道德规范建设,为全面提高高等教育质量尤其是研究生培养质量做出贡献。

多年来,北京大学不断探索提高研究生培养质量的途径,并进行了卓有成效的研究生培养机制改革,取得了一些成果,收获了一些经验。为进一步了解国外大学教育制度和研究生培养情况,吸收他们的先进经验,北京大学研究生院与北京大学出版社共同遴选了一批在国外具有较广泛影响的教材和参考书,并正式出版了"学术道德与学术规范系列丛书"。该丛书中每种著作针对一个主题,分别从学术道德、文献搜集、研究资讯的管理、阅读和写作指导、科研计划的撰写、论文写作与发表及科学研究的基本方法等方面,介绍国际学术研究的基本规范程式。与此同时,在课程教学积累的基础上,一批由北京大学教师编著的研究生学术规范类教材也正在逐步完成。它们凝聚了北大教师们多年的研究经验和成果,也是与中国教育实际契合的很好的教学科研用书。这套丛书给广大研究生和研究生教育工作者们打开了一扇世界之窗,有利于我们的学生和教育工作者借鉴国内外学术规范和学术研究的先进方法,吸取更多的经验和教训,有利于提高我国高校教育质量和自主创新能立,促生更多具有国际先进水平的学术成果和更健全的教育体系。

"工欲善其事,必先利其器"。加强学术规范教育和训练是我国研究生教育长期的课程和目标,良好的学术规范是科学研究的基础,也是全面提高学生培养质量的有力保证,从规范入手,让学生知道如何规范地搞科研、做学问,自觉遵守学术道德,恪守科学精神,对推动我国研究生教育有深远意义。我愿意和广大教育工作者们一起,从关注基础、关注规范入手,不断提升研究生教育的质量,形成研究生教育立足规范、注重质量、追求卓越、勇于创新的新气象。

PREFACE

Why did I write this book? Three main reasons come to mind. The first is that, for many years, I have worked with colleagues and postgraduate students whose first language is Chinese. We struggled to prepare manuscripts for submission to ISI[①]-listed journals. Over time, I found that specific problems kept reappearing, and decided to make our work easier by documenting how you can avoid these difficulties. Second, while many manuals give excellent advice on how to perfect a final draft, few (I have not found any) approach the horrible problem of writing the first draft, especially when English is not your mother tongue. The third reason is that I cannot be sure that I have anything useful to say until I write it down and see that it still makes sense.

What can you expect to learn by reading this book? I want you to learn how to communicate your findings to academics around the world, in English, in such a simple and direct way that they cannot fail to immediately understand what you mean, and appreciate the clarity of your style of thinking and writing. The focus is on simple language, short sentences, logical organization, and avoiding vagueness and confusion. You can learn no fancy tricks here. My viewpoint is that good biomedical writing is understandable by any educated person. I recall with affection a comment made by a fellow neurophysiologist about a particularly difficult paper written by a prominent

---

[①] The Institute for Scientific Information is at http://www.isiwebofknowledge.com/.

colleague: *If you can't be sure, be obscure*. That is to say, if a paper is very difficult to understand, it is likely that the authors do not really know what they are talking about, and the paper will probably be ignored. After all, if the data are really important, someone who comprehends them better will write a version that all of us can understand.

In short, my goal is that after you have read this little book, you will be able to write easily, clearly and concisely about your work, and that readers (especially journal editors and reviewers) will immediately understand what you mean.

Iain C. Bruce

[icbruce@zju.edu.cn]

Hangzhou, June 2011.

ACKNOWLEDGEMENTS

After a presentation to a group of *Talented Youth of Zhejiang Province*, one participant asked: *How can I learn to write like you?* My answer went something like this: Two early influences molded my brain for writing. First, my grandmother, Aggie Bruce, read to me when I was bedridden in childhood, which was often. So, my developing brain absorbed the rich language of stories from the 19th century—such classics as *Black Beauty* and *Treasure Island*. Then, the harsh but effective education system of Scotland in the 1950s and 1960s forced the rules of *proper* English into my head. So, my answer was, first, choose your grandparents carefully, and second, learn from tough teachers.

More recent influences led directly to this book. I am indebted to my colleague and friend XIA Qiang of Zhejiang University School of Medicine, who in 1995 had the imagination to challenge me to teach his students how to write papers. This was a humbling experience, making me realize that although I write reasonably well, trying to pass this skill on to others is not easy. After the first attempts, further development of writing workshops was supported and encouraged with forward thinking by Johan KARLBERG, Director of the Clinical Trials Centre at the University of Hong Kong, with great enthusiasm by ZHOU Zhuan at the Institute of Molecular Medicine, Peking University, and with his dedication to promoting international communication by Paul POON of the Department of Physiology, National

Cheng Kung University College of Medicine. Without their encouragement, my interest in teaching students how to write would certainly have evaporated. Always in the background, but most important to me, are the generations of postgraduate research students, especially those at the University of Hong Kong, Zhejiang University School of Medicine, and Peking University, who served as guinea-pigs in my attempts at teaching, helped me to understand their difficulties, and whose successes continue to provide my primary job satisfaction. Last but certainly not least, I wish to thank my charming and talented wife, Ping Ting LAM, who is herself an established writer in the Chinese language, for her constant support.

Note: This kind of book requires the use of many quotation marks; to save space and ink, I have simply used *italics* to indicate quotations. * Since this book has developed from live lectures, I use *CAPITALIZED ITALICS* to indicate that I am shouting at you.

Iain C. Bruce,

[icbruce@zju.edu.cn]

Hangzhou, June 2011.

---

* I sympathize with the statement from Treble HA, Valkins GH (1936) *An ABC of English Usage*. Oxford University Press: *It is remarkable in an age particularly contemptuous of punctuation marks that we have not yet had the courage to abolish inverted commas... After all, they are a modern invention. The Bible is plain enough without them; and so is the literature of the 18th century. Bernard Shaw scorns them. However, since they are with us, we must do our best with them, trying always to reduce them to a minimum.* I found this quotation in Cooper BM (1964) *Writing Technical Reports*. Penguin Books, p.76.

中文序一

Iain Bruce 教授总结 20 多年来他在中国内地、香港和台湾开设生物医学专业论文英语写作课程的教案和心得，写成《生命科学论文写作指南》一书，该书由北京大学出版社出版。听到这一消息，我感到非常高兴。

根据新近中国科学技术信息研究所发布的 2010 年中国科技论文统计结果，2010 年以我国研究机构作者为第一作者发表的国际论文有 12.15 万篇，居全球第二。其中有 23968 篇论文（约 19.7%）发表后的引用次数超过其所在学科的平均水平。而这近 2.4 万篇论文中，81.6% 来自高校。随着中国对外开放，英语作为科技界国际学术交流的通用语言，愈发显得重要。而目前我国的英语教学方式存在问题。学生从小学到大学，虽然花费了大量的时间学英语，不少学生即便过了大学英语六级考试、托福和 GRE，甚至考得高分，但还是开不了口，写不好一段短文。不少研究生常为写一篇学位论文的英语论文摘要，或国际学术会议的报告摘要而发愁。我国学者所写的论文因英语太差而被退回的也屡有所闻。在此情况下，一批专门代人修改英语论文的网络公司也应运而生。

Bruce 教授在他的教学实践中，十分理解一个英语不是母语的人，在撰写英语论文初稿时所面临的困难。科技论文要求文字简洁明了、表达精确。作者在书中通过大量的实例，让读者知道如何入手准备生物科技论文初稿，如何编辑修改，如何防范学术不端情况的发生，从而使你的论文的读者，特别是杂志编辑及审稿人，可以明白无误地理解你在论文中所讲的研究结果和表达的意思。希望本书的出版能使更多的年轻学者和研究生从中得益,以不断提高自己的英语写作水平,并能更好地用英语与国外同行进行学术交流。

许智宏

2011年12月写于燕园

中文序二

当今,科学技术是第一生产力。新近从中国科技部获悉,1998年以来中国对科学技术研究经费投入平均年增长20%以上。2010年中国SCI论文总数已位列世界第二,仅次于美国。不仅论文数量迅猛增加,中国研究论文的质量也大幅提高。以心血管基础研究为例,2004年中国(除香港、澳门和台湾地区外)在该领域旗舰期刊之一——Circulation Research上近乎没有论文。2010年该刊发表了至少10篇来自中国(除香港、澳门和台湾地区外)的论文,超越意大利。中国改革开放30年来(对于生命科学特别是过去10年来),我国学者取得这些骄人进步非常不易。我们大家为此付出了艰辛努力,并克服了重重困难。除了东西方共有的"常规"科研挑战(智慧和毅力),我们还有非常规的语言屏障。因为当今世界科技语言使用英语,这对中文为母语的我国学者投往高影响力SCI期刊的论文是严重的挑战。所幸,在我国生命科学走向世界的过程中,我们得到了一批西方友人的大力帮助,使得我们把一批重要科研成果及时发表到国际权威期刊成为可能。原香港大学教授,现任浙江大学教授和北京大学访问教授的Iain Bruce就是其中突出代表。

我于1996年获得中科院首批"百人计划"资助,次年回国组建实验室。至2002年,实验室有一批论文期待发表到有影响力的期刊(包括中国科学院神经所提倡的"七大期刊")。但是一经投稿,便无一例外的遭遇审稿人无情的批评,指示论文需"native English speaker"科学同行专家阅读和copy-editing修改。所幸,在生理学会常务理事会上,我偶然从浙江大学夏强教授处探得"良方"。经他介绍,我与Iain相识。从此,我实验室发表的几乎全部 SCI 论文,以及我的一些同事和朋友的论文持续不断地得到了 Iain 的专业修改。据不完全统计,2006 年以来,仅他做 copy-editing 修改的北京大学的生命学科论文就有 200 多篇,其中有 110 余篇在 SCI 期刊发表,平均影响因子 >4(包括 3 篇"CNS",20 余篇 PNAS 以上高端期刊)。Iain 对北大生命科学论文发表作出了显著贡献。

2010 年时值 Iain 在北大分子医学研究所任访问教授和从事北大英文写作教学 5 周年,我们建议他将 20 多年来在香港大学、台湾成功大学、浙江大学和北京大学开设的生物学专业论文英语写作课程的教案和心得总结成书。现在,在北大研究生院和分子医学研究所的大力帮助下,Iain Bruce 终于完成《生命科学论文写作指南》,经北京大学出版社出版,希望在更大范围对中国从事生命科学研究者的英文写作有所帮助。

周专,北京大学分子医学研究所
2011 年 12 月 13 日

中文序三

在目前学术界 publish or perish 的压力之下，我与周专教授深有同感：中国人向有国际影响力的学术刊物投稿，难免遇到语言障碍的困扰。我有时受年轻朋友和研究生之邀，帮他们对文稿进行文字润色或加工，也常有力不从心的惭愧。Iain Bruce 教授在北京大学分子医学研究所为研究生讲授"生命科学英文论文写作方法"时，我常去旁听，很受教益，但由于种种原因，我从未能听全过，很是遗憾。今闻 Bruce 教授将他在中国教学二十余年的成果和经验总结成书，即将出版；又受分子医学研究所程和平教授之邀，让我说说个人向 Iain 学习的情况，实在不胜荣幸。欣然握笔，谈谈我的个人体会和心得。

Iain 不仅全面系统地向读者阐明国际科学论文"八股"IMRAD 的内容、要求与规范，突出了该书应有的实用性，而且还试图用自己的个人经验帮助初学者从一开始就建立起良好的写作习惯和规矩。其中有些恰与我的个人经验不谋而合，如开始起草文稿时用纸和笔，不用计算机，特别使我对该书倍感亲切。

书的内容丰富翔实，对许多问题的处理与分析远非仅限于作者个人的经验与偏爱，而多是引经据典，根据正统的文献和历史娓娓道来，使你对他所传授的学问、知识和技巧深信不疑，又体现了作者在科技语言方面的理论水平。

作者说：他从小受到的教育就是不可用"and"来开始一句话，并且对此始终奉为经典，认真恪守。我也从学生时代就被告知，科学论文的文字必须严谨规范，不得有口语化的色彩和倾向，因为那是作者科学态度不够严肃的表现。但是 Iain 从人类语言的发展历程出发,论述了语言和文体本来就是时代的产物和反映,天然应当是可变的,体现了他在语言学方面的造诣和修养。他还以 Dawkins 为实例,说明时尚的语言表达并不一定损害科学性和严肃性,使我懂得了应当抱有不断学习和变革的态度,免于因循守旧、抱残守缺。

我期待这本书的出版,因为它是一本雅俗共赏的工具书,使人学到有用的知识和技术。又因为它能启发深思,使人悟到"活到老、学到老"的治学和做人的正确态度。我还深信,它将是新书市场上的一本畅销书。

顾孝诚,北京大学生命科学学院

2011 年 12 月 14 日

CONTENTS

INTRODUCTION	1
GENERAL ENGLISH AND BIOMEDICAL ENGLISH	3
THERAPEUTIC VALUE OF WRITING	5
CHAPTER 1 GETTING STARTED: METHODS OF REDUCING THE PAIN	7
CHECK THE WEB SITE OF YOUR INTERNATIONAL SOCIETY	10
USE SIMPLE ENGLISH	12
DEVELOP A WRITING HABIT	14
WRITING IS ONE THING AND EDITING IS ANOTHER	15
DEVELOP A READING HABIT	17
KEEP AN EVERYDAY BOOK	20
CHAPTER 2 WRITING THE FIRST DRAFT	25
USE PEN AND PAPER	28
THE RADMI SEQUENCE	29
RESULTS AND DISCUSSION	30
METHODS	31
INTRODUCTION	32
CHAPTER 3 EDITING THE FIRST DRAFT	39
RESULTS	41
DISCUSSION	44

METHODS	48
INTRODUCTION	52
INSTRUCTIONS FOR AUTHORS	53

CHAPTER 4 COMMON ERRORS: ITEMS TO DELETE FROM YOUR FIRST DRAFT AND AVOID FOREVER AFTER …… 59

ABBREVIATIONS	61
ADMINISTRATE	62
APOSTROPHES	63
BACK-TRANSLATION	64
CAN/COULD	65
COMMON THINGS ARE NOT NECESSARILY POPULAR	68
DETECTING OR MEASURING?	69
EQUIPMENTS, RESEARCHES, EVIDENCES	70
ETC/AND SO ON	71
EXPENDABLE PHRASES	73
INCLUDING	74
NOUN STRINGS	76
OBSERVED	77
OBVIOUSLY	78
OUT-OF-DATE/INAPPROPRIATE TERMINOLOGY	81
RESPECTIVELY	83
SENTENCE INVERSION	86
SIGNIFICANTLY	87
TENSES	96
THE PROBLEM OF *THE*	97

CONTENTS

THERE IS... 99
TILDE (~) 100
USE IS USEFUL 101
WITH OR BY? 102

CHAPTER 5   POTENTIAL DANGERS: ETHICS AND PLAGIARISM 103

ETHICS 105
PLAGIARISM 108

CHAPTER 6   OTHER THINGS 113

ABSTRACT 115
ACKNOWLEDGEMENTS 117
COVER LETTER 117
FIGURE LEGENDS (CAPTIONS) 119
KEYWORDS 120
NAMES 122
REFERENCES 122
THESIS/DISSERTATION 126
TITLE 127
WORD PROCESSORS: Chinese *versus* English 129

FINAL WORDS 133
APPENDIX I   SELECTED ADVICE FROM *INSTRUCTIONS FOR AUTHORS* 137
APPENDIX II   TOP JOURNALS 153

目 录

简介 ··· 1

第1章　入门：减轻痛苦的方法 ·· 7

第2章　撰写初稿 ·· 25

第3章　编辑初稿 ·· 39

第4章　常见错误：从初稿中删除并且以后要永远避免

　　　　出现的错误 ··· 59

第5章　潜在的危险：道德和剽窃 ··································· 103

第6章　其他事宜 ··· 113

结语 ··· 133

附录1　一些给作者的建议 ·· 137

附录2　顶尖杂志列表 ·· 153

INTRODUCTION

>>
GENERAL ENGLISH AND BIOMEDICAL ENGLISH
THERAPEUTIC VALUE OF WRITING
  >

INTRODUCTION

*The art of writing is the art of applying the seat of one's trousers to the seat of one's chair*①

GENERAL ENGLISH AND BIOMEDICAL ENGLISH

General English is more difficult to use than biomedical English—for a biomedical investigator, it is easier to discuss a clinical case or an experiment than to make conversation on a topic like recent movies or the economy. In biomedical English, the language is simple and direct with its own specific terms, while in general English, difficult colloquialisms and careless, imprecise statements are routinely used. I encourage you to focus on using English when discussing your experiments and your clinical experiences—this is easier to master than the peculiarities of ordinary conversation. Similarly, writing biomedical English is easier than writing to a friend who is not familiar with research. The biomedical style is based on a formula (the IMRAD formula: Introduction, Methods, Results and Discussion②), the content is structured, and the vocabulary is restricted. Form a Biomedical English Club with your colleagues for practicing the kind

---

① In other words, *JUST SIT DOWN AND WRITE*. Kingsley Amis (1922-1995) wrote more than 20 novels, including *Lucky Jim*, as well as books of criticism, short stories, scripts and poetry. http://en.wikipedia.org/wiki/Kingsley_Amis.

② A study of four of the major medical journals, the *British Medical Journal*, the *Journal of the American Medical Association*, *The Lancet*, and the *New England Journal of Medicine*, found that the IMRAD formula began to be used in the 1940s, reached 80% in the 1970s, and has been the only pattern since the 1980s. http://www.pubmedcentral.nih.gov/articlerender.fcgi?artid=442179.

of discussion of your ideas and data that you are likely to have when you attend an international conference.

In biomedical writing, you can ignore many of the rules of English that you learned in school, especially the complexities of verb tenses (simple, continuous, perfect, and perfect continuous forms of past, present, and future③). You need not waste energy searching for alternatives to simple words like *increased*, just to provide variety (such as *aggrandized*, *augmented*, *elevated*, *enhanced*, *exacerbated*...). Your reader just wants the facts and is irritated by having to search for the meanings of obscure synonyms. *Roget's Thesaurus*④ and its equivalents are helpful but also dangerous. I was recently amazed by a Thesaurus-user who threw the term *obnubilate* at me in a manuscript. After a search, I learned that it means *obscure* or *cloudy*. Furthermore, the style of English usage changes with time (compare Charles Darwin's English with that of Richard Dawkins). I was trained, for example, never to begin a sentence with *and*. As a result, I never do and probably never will. Recently, however, biomedical writers have broken this rule, so beginning a sentence with *and* (when it is closely linked to the previous sentence) is becoming increasingly common. Since one of the best biomedical writers (Richard Dawkins) commits this "crime" in a recent book⑤, who am I to object? Such changes simply reflect the fact that language is a product of the human brain and changes to meet its needs. What is correct English? It is the way educated people use the language now.

---

③ http://www.englishpage.com/verbpage/verbtenseintro.html.
④ *Roget's Thesaurus of English Words and Phrases* (2004). G Davidson (Ed), Penguin Books.
⑤ Dawkins R. (2006) *The God Delusion*. Houghton Mifflin Co., Boston. A biologist of renown, Dawkins was the first holder of the Charles Simonyi Chair for the Public Understanding of Science at the University of Oxford (1995-2008).

THERAPEUTIC VALUE OF WRITING

No matter where in the world you work, this is a stressful time to be a young investigator. I hear of unreasonable demands by supervisors, near impossible requirements for promotion, too many hours of teaching (increasingly in English), publish (in English) or perish, and the lack of time to lead a reasonably normal life outside the lab or clinic. During periods of great stress, I help myself to stay sane by keeping a secret notebook in which I write down thoughts about the situation. A news item in *Scientific American*[6] briefly outlines evidence for the benefits of writing to deal with stress. The benefits listed include memory improvement, better sleep patterns, and boosting the immune system. These findings are based on investigations not only of patients coping with diseases such as cancer and AIDS, but also normal university students. So, you may wish to *kill two birds with one stone*[7] by starting your own secret stress-reduction notebook in English. Of course, this is not a new idea in China. Wang Yi (89-158 AD), imperial librarian and commentator during the Eastern Han dynasty, was *a great believer in the therapeutic value of creative writing*[8].

So, to encourage your further development as a biomedical writer, Chapter 1 *Getting Started: Methods of Reducing the Pain* provides a series of

---

[6] *Scientific American*, June, 2008, page 32. http://www.sciam.com.

[7] According to WikiAnswers.com, this common English phrase originated from the Chinese saying *yi shi er niao* (one stone two birds).

[8] Minford J., Lau JSM (Eds) (2000) *Classical Chinese Literature: An Anthology of Translations. Volume I: From Antiquity to the Tang dynasty*. The Chinese University of Hong Kong Press, Hong Kong, p.39.

helpful hints—simple things you can do to prepare yourself to write effectively. Chapter 2, *Writing the First Draft*, focuses on the most difficult part—getting everything down on paper or screen using the RADMI (Results and Discussion, Methods, Introduction) sequence. This chapter contains an exercise aimed at illustrating the special principles behind generating a first draft. Chapters 3 and 4 are devoted to editing the first and subsequent drafts, with emphasis on the particular problems faced by a writer whose mother tongue is one of the many varieties of Chinese. In Chapter 5, the potential dangers arising from ethical requirements in biomedical research and the problem of plagiarism, especially in relation to the ease of access to information on the internet along with cutting and pasting, are briefly covered. Chapter 6 ends the book with suggestions about important details not included in the IMRAD formula.

CHAPTER 1

GETTING STARTED:
METHODS OF REDUCING THE PAIN
>>>

>>
CHECK THE WEB SITE OF YOUR INTERNATIONAL SOCIETY
USE SIMPLE ENGLISH
DEVELOP A WRITING HABIT
WRITING IS ONE THING AND EDITING IS ANOTHER
DEVELOP A READING HABIT
KEEP AN EVERYDAY BOOK
>

CHAPTER 1　GETTING STARTED: METHODS OF REDUCING THE PAIN

A journey of 1,000 li begins with a single step[9]

The most difficult thing in writing, for me, is getting the first words down on the page. The painting by the Norwegian artist Edvard Munch, *The Scream*[10], illustrates how I feel when I have to begin a new piece of writing. Over many years, I have found no easy way—you just have to decide: *I will start this paper now*. The only good advice I can give to you, and the most difficult to follow, is not to wait until the deadline is near. Start now! Time passes quickly; although the deadline seems distant, it is not. *START WRITING NOW*! Even if you have not done any experiments yet, you can begin an outline of the reasons why the project you are starting is worthwhile, what gap in our knowledge it fills, or what hypothesis you plan to test. *TIME IS SHORT, GET GOING*!

The Scream

---

[9]　Lao Zi (6th century BC), author of the *Dao De Jing*.
[10]　http://www.edvard-munch.com.

CHECK THE WEB SITE OF YOUR INTERNATIONAL SOCIETY

Go to the web site of the major academic society in your field and look for useful information about writing in your specialty. If such a resource is not available, suggest to your Society that it should develop one, or at least provide useful links. For example, the National Institutes of Health (USA) provides a list of sites for biomedical writing[11], and the Medical Research Council (UK) has a brief article entitled *The secrets of good science writing*[12]. Worth special mention is the publishing company *Elsevier*, which is especially active in assisting authors in China to prepare and submit papers for publication[13]. For example, on Elsevier's webpage in the section *How to write a scientific article*, *Author Pack 2*, you can find the following comments on style and language:

It is important to refer to the journal's guide for authors' notes on style. Some authors write their article with a specific journal in mind, while others write the article and then adapt it to fit the style of a journal they subsequently choose. Regardless of your preference, some fundamentals remain true throughout the process of writing a scientific article. The object is to report your findings and conclusions clearly, and as concisely as possible; try to avoid embellishment with unnecessary words or phrases. The use of the active voice will

---

[11] http://www.training.nih.gov/careers/careercenter/publish.html.
[12] http://www.mrc.ac.uk/sciencesociety/Awards/Sciencewriting/index.htm.
[13] http://www.paperpub.com.cn.

CHAPTER 1 GETTING STARTED: METHODS OF REDUCING THE PAIN

shorten sentence length. For example, <u>carbon dioxide was consumed by the plant</u>... is in the passive voice. By changing to the active voice it can be shortened to <u>the plant consumed carbon dioxide</u>... The following shows how tenses are most often used in science writing:

For known facts and hypotheses, the present tense should be used.

' The average life expectancy of a honey bee is 6 weeks. '

When you refer to experiments you have conducted, the past tense should be used.

' All the honey bees were maintained in an environment with a consistent temperature of 23°C. '

When you describe the results of an experiment, the past tense should be used.

' The average life span of bees in our contained environment was 8 weeks. '

Commercial editing companies sometimes provide helpful information and even free courses. For example, the course outline provided by *Inter-Biotec* states:

This free course is designed to help you successfully publish biomedical papers in English. It provides a full outline of the preparation of manuscripts with regards to planning, style, structure and composition.

Specific reference to correct English usage is made, and important factors to consider when submitting and publishing papers are covered[14].

---

[14] http://www.inter-biotec.com/biowc/biowc.html.

USE SIMPLE ENGLISH (short words, short sentences)

The *Plain English Campaign*⑮ is worth a visit for examples of clear English and gobbledygook [this is a lovely word; it sounds just like its meaning—*something described in an overly complex, incoherent, or incomprehensible manner*]. To quote from the Campaign's home page:

Since 1979, we have been campaigning against gobbledygook, jargon and misleading public information. We have helped many government departments and other official organisations with their documents, reports and publications. We believe that everyone should have access to clear and concise information.

An excellent example of incomprehensible writing was reported in the amusing and thought-provoking journal, the *Annals of Improbable Research*⑯. Readers were challenged to summarize the following published statement in seven words:

"*Specifically, I have been concerned with the processes by which individuals construct and enact motivational 'agendas for action' that draw upon and integrate features of their personal identities and their social settings, and that guide and direct their pursuit of relevant life outcomes in diverse domains of functioning.*" [This was written by a professor of psychology in the USA.]

Here is the judges' pick for Best Seven-Word Translation:

"*Why do people do what they do?*"

---

⑮ http://www.plainenglish.co.uk/
⑯ http://www.improbable.com/magazine/#IssuesOnline.

CHAPTER 1　GETTING STARTED: METHODS OF REDUCING THE PAIN

■ EXAMPLE[17]

Here is an abstract with many shortcomings, including the use of unnecessarily complex words:

There are well known effects of acupuncture at point A on cardiovascular illnesses. We try to elucidate some of the underlying mechanisms in such actions, by means of repetitive electrostimulation of the point, comparing the results with those obtained by stimuli on extra-acupunctural point, and over the median nerve. We find significative modifications of the cardiac frequency and the systolic blood pressure after stimulus at A. No demonstrable effects were attributable to the mere repetitive stimulation nor the median nerve stimulation. [81 words]

What does *modifications of the cardiac frequency* mean? It means *changes in heart rate*. Why not say so? [Actually, we would like to know whether the rate increased or decreased. Telling us that the heart rate changed is not telling us much.] The way this abstract is written suggests a lack of clear thinking about the results—the only conclusion we can draw from the facts presented in the abstract is that the cardiovascular effects are specific to the acupuncture point. No data on *underlying mechanisms* are presented. A clearer version might be something like this:

---

[17]　In this and all the following examples. The incorrect statement is in italics and comes first, while the corrected version is in normal type amd comes second.

> *Acupuncture at point A benefits patients with heart disease, but the details are not clear* [Introduction]. *We therefore set out to determine whether stimulation at this point affected parameters of cardiovascular function by comparing the results of stimulation at the point, a nearby region of skin, and the median nerve* [Methods]. *Heart rate increased/decreased, while systolic pressure increased/decreased after stimulation at point A, but these parameters were unchanged by stimulation at the other locations* [Results]. *Therefore, the effects of acupuncture on the cardiovascular system are specific to point A* [Conclusion]. [86 words]

DEVELOP A WRITING HABIT

Write at a regular time, for a fixed time. Before you say *Impossible, I have no free time*! Let us make this goal achievable: even if you begin by writing for only 5 minutes every day after breakfast (say, 100 words), you will accumulate a satisfying amount of material in a month (~3,000 words is the length of a short paper). If you then make this habit part of your life, and gradually extend your writing time to 30 minutes, then to an hour, you become an efficient and prolific writer. One of my former colleagues has this habit, and envious friends joke that he must write with both hands and both feet at the same time to publish so many papers.

The next time you are waiting for something, maybe later today, do not play with your cellphone, or just watch the world go by; take out your notebook and start writing something—anything. Even if you only write a

CHAPTER 1   GETTING STARTED: METHODS OF REDUCING THE PAIN

few sentences, when you have this habit, the sentences, paragraphs, and pages accumulate with relatively little effort.

Ernest Hemingway[18], famous for his concise style, lived an unconventional life. But during the periods when he was writing, he lived like a monk. *Mr. Hemingway works on a strict schedule that produces an average of 500 to 1,000 words a day. 'I start in at seven in the morning,' he says, 'and I always quit when I'm going good, so that I'll be able to pick right up again the next day'.*[19] It is unlikely that many of these 500 to 1,000 words per day actually survived to appear in the final novel. He would have severely edited his daily production. I do not suggest that you try to be like Hemingway, but learn from his writing habit: write a lot and then edit it.

Consider this: if you plan a career in the academic world, you will have to spend much of your working life writing in English (grant proposals, patent applications, papers, letters, books, lecture notes...). The sooner you start, the better.

WRITING IS ONE THING AND EDITING IS ANOTHER

A common problem seen when a young investigator begins to write goes something like this. The investigator writes a few sentences, thinks about them, finds an error in spelling or grammar, and then goes back to correct it. He or she then returns to write a few more lines, goes back to make corrections, and so the alternating pattern continues. The train of thought is

---

[18]   Pulitzer Prize for *The Old Man and the Sea* in 1953, and Nobel Prize for Literature in 1954.
[19]   From: *On the Books* by Roger Bourne Linscott, reprinted in *Conversation with Ernest Hemingway*, edited by Matthew J. Bruccoli. http://www.timelesshemingway.com/faq/faq5.shtml#words.

constantly being broken to correct trivial errors. It takes a long time and a lot of effort to generate a paragraph in this way.

Writing requires you to maintain a train of thought, to use your imagination, and to make connections between your results and published work. The parts of your brain essential for these skills lie mainly in the right hemisphere, which is not good at putting items in logical order, getting the grammar right, or spelling words correctly. Concentration is energy-consuming, so creative writing is best done when you and your right hemisphere are feeling fresh. In contrast, editing what you write requires knowledge of grammar and syntax, an adequate vocabulary, and a sense of logical order (left hemisphere). Since the two jobs of writing and editing depend on different areas, and the brain works best solving one problem at a time, the jobs should be performed separately. Alternating between writing and editing (from right to left hemisphere and back again) is very slow and inefficient. Multitasking merely reduces the efficiency with which each task is performed[20].

When you are writing, do nothing but write—fill the pages with words until you cannot think of anything more to say. By all means, begin with the intention of, say, writing the Introduction, and write your train of thought (so long as it does not wander off into fantasies about your attractive classmate); do not be concerned about logical order, grammar or spelling. Ideas pop up, seemingly at random—write them down as they happen. If you do not capture them now, they may be lost forever. At a later time, perhaps when you have run out of ideas and are tired, spell-check and cut-and-paste the

---

[20] Dux PE, Ivanoff J., Asplund CL, Marois R. (2006) Isolation of a central bottleneck of information processing with time-resolved fMRI. *Neuron* 52, 1109-1120. The authors conclude: *These results suggest that a neural network of frontal lobe areas acts as a central bottleneck of information processing that severely limits our ability to multitask.*

material you produced, using your logical and grammatical left hemisphere.

Predominantly left hemisphere functions	Predominantly right hemisphere functions
ANALYSIS	CREATIVITY
GRAMMAR	PARALLEL PROCESSING
LOGIC	PATTERN RECOGNITION
REASONING	RHYTHM
SERIAL PROCESSING	SYNTHESIS
SPELLING	VISUAL IMAGERY

Functions associated with the right hemisphere include pattern recognition, rhythm, visual imagery, creativity, parallel processing, and synthesis. These functions underlie creative writing (that is, writing the first draft). Functions associated with the left hemisphere include logic, reasoning, mathematics, spelling, grammar, serial or linear processing, and analysis. These are functions needed when editing your work.[21]

DEVELOP A READING HABIT

Perhaps the most effective way to improve your writing style is to read clear, informative, and concise English in and around your field of study. In recent years, increasing numbers of professional scientists have moved away from laboratory work to take up careers as science journalists. They are skilled writers who also have a deep understanding of their topics. I am filled with admiration when I read a summary of new findings reported at the annual meetings of organizations like the *Society for Neuroscience* (more

---

[21] An entry to the field of hemispheric specialization is: *Splitting the Human Brain* at http://www.indiana.edu/~pietsch/split-brain.html.

than 16,300 presentations and posters, and 32,186 attendees at the 2007 meeting[22]). The ability to digest the key information in a few days and summarize it in a few paragraphs is remarkable. You can read their work in such popular science magazines as *Discover*[23], *New Scientist*[24], and *Scientific American*[25]. Furthermore, the *News and Views* section in *Nature*[26] and the *Perspectives* section in *Science*[27] are not only informative, but also provide excellent examples of clear and concise English. Finally, a few especially talented individuals have served society by popularizing science—making difficult concepts accessible to the general public. In the biomedical area, such figures include Richard Dawkins[28], Stephen Jay Gould[29], Peter Medawar[30] and Lewis Thomas[31]. Much can be learned from them.

Whenever you can, READ ALOUD to yourself. Do this with textbooks, important papers, and your own writing. This will help you to become more familiar and comfortable with English, both written and spoken. This may seem like a childish thing to do, but it makes sense. After all, spoken language developed by our ancestors at least 100,000 years ago and has been used ever since as the primary form of communication. Language was first

---

[22] Neuroscience Quarterly, Fall 2008, page iv.
[23] http://discovermagazine.com/
[24] http://www.newscientist.com/home.ns.
[25] http://www.sciam.com/
[26] http://www.nature.com/index.html.
[27] http://www.sciencemag.org/
[28] Dawkins R (1989) *The Selfish Gene*. Second Edition, Oxford University Press, is perhaps the most important book in the life sciences of the 20th century. Others of great value include *The Extended Phenotype* (1982), *The Blind Watchmaker* (1986), *Climbing Mount Improbable* (1996), and *The Ancestor's Tale* (2004).
[29] Gould SJ (2002) *I Have Landed*. Harmony Books, New York, is the last of his collections of brilliant essays on the life sciences, and includes a list of all previous collections.
[30] Medawar PB (1979) *Advice to a Young Scientist*. Harper and Row, New York.
[31] Thomas L (1985) *Late Night Thoughts*. Oxford University Press, and (1983) *The Youngest Science: Notes of a Medicine-Watcher*. Viking Press.

CHAPTER 1 GETTING STARTED: METHODS OF REDUCING THE PAIN

written down less than 10,000 years ago, and since then has been restricted to a few privileged groups of people (mainly priests, to make prayers permanent, and businessmen, to record deals), until just a few centuries ago, when literacy began to spread to all classes. We learn the spoken language automatically but have to go to school to learn reading and writing. So, presumably, much brain space is devoted dealing with the spoken form. Ancient Chinese scholars always read out loud while preparing for the imperial examinations, and today I see undergraduates on campus at Peking and Zhejiang universities pacing up and down, reading aloud from their English textbooks. They are doing the right thing!

[I know, you don't have time for this. I suggest you try to make time; such reading not only improves your writing but also expands your general knowledge and helps you to generate new ideas. You may benefit from a variety of time-management resources available on the internet.[32] Wikipedia defines time management as: *the act or process of exercising conscious control over the amount of time spent on specific activities, especially to increase efficiency or productivity. Time management may be aided by a range of skills, tools, and techniques used to manage time when accomplishing specific tasks, projects and goals. This set encompasses a wide scope of activities, and these include planning, allocating, setting goals, delegation, analysis of time spent, monitoring, organizing, scheduling, and prioritizing. Initially, time management referred to just business or work activities, but eventually the term broadened to include personal activities as well. A time management system is a designed combination of processes, tools, techniques, and methods. Usually time management is a necessity in any project development as it determines the project completion time and scope.*[33]]

---

[32] Such as http://www.mindtools.com/pages/main/newMN_HTE.htm.
[33] http://en.wikipedia.org/wiki/Time_management.

KEEP AN EVERYDAY BOOK

Many of you were probably told to keep something like an Everyday Book in primary school, when you were learning to write in Chinese. This involved keeping a notebook of characters you had not seen before, descriptive or poetic phrases, and famous quotations from literature. Your teacher inspected these efforts to confirm that you were reading good stuff after class. When it was no longer required, you stopped doing this. I encourage you to revive the habit of using an Everyday Book; the intention is not to please your teachers, but to develop your skills in writing biomedical English. You already spend a lot of time reading papers in your field and making notes on relevant techniques, data and interpretations. These notes are kept in a References notebook or file, which you use as a source of ideas and information when writing your manuscript. The papers you read also contain another important kind of information—how to write publishable scientific English. Open another notebook or file for terms and phrases you can use when describing and discussing your project.

When reading papers, have a good English dictionary by your side or on screen[34] (not English to Chinese unless absolutely necessary) and do not allow any word to pass unless you know its exact meaning. An up-to-date medical dictionary is essential.[35] Build up your own Everyday Book of useful words and phrases appropriate for your field (taking care that you do not

---

[34] Such as Merriam-Webster Online, http://www.m-w.com/home.htm.
[35] One is at MerckSource, http://www.mercksource.com/pp/us/cns/cns_home.jsp.

CHAPTER 1　GETTING STARTED: METHODS OF REDUCING THE PAIN

accidentally commit plagiarism). The top international journals in each field, where the papers are probably (but not necessarily) written well, are identified in the *Journal Citation Reports* published in the *Science Citation Index*.[36] [See Appendix II for examples.]

■ EXAMPLES

> I made the following list in about 30 minutes, by pulling a journal off the shelf and looking through several Introduction, Methods, Results and Discussion sections.
>
> Phrases from the Introduction:
>
> *Based on an analysis of... the authors concluded that...*
>
> *The animal models, together with the human studies, demonstrate that...*
>
> *Previous studies did not reveal... This uncertainty has prompted speculation that...*
>
> *Moreover, recent studies of... have raised questions about...*
>
> *Relatively little is known about the mechanisms underlying...*
>
> *The present study focuses on...*
>
> *We undertook this project because very little is known about...*
>
> *The specific goals of this experiment were to determine whether..., and, if so whether...*
>
> *On the basis of initial studies... Recent studies, however, revealed that...*

---

[36]　http://www.isiwebofknowledge.com/

Here we investigated this question by... This technique offered the possibility of detecting...

We showed recently that... We argued on the basis of our findings that... These findings led us to compare...

Phrases from the Methods:

Experiments with animals followed protocols approved by the Animal Care and Use Committees of our institutions.

Drug injection was performed as previously described (ref.). Briefly, animals were anesthetized...

Standard gene targeting techniques were used to...

Two-way repeated measures ANOVA was conducted to assess the effects of... Repeated measures one-way ANOVA was also conducted to assess the effects of... Dunnett's multiple comparison post-test was performed to compare...

Fifteen volunteers were recruited by... All participants gave informed consent.

XY mice at 4-6 weeks were obtained from...

Phrases from the Results:

To test whether...
We next examined whether...
We consistently saw...
Based on these results, we...
To further examine the hypothesis that...

CHAPTER 1 GETTING STARTED: METHODS OF REDUCING THE PAIN

> Phrases from the Discussion:
>
> *The most important new conclusion of this study is that...*
>
> *Contrary to our expectation, this study shows that increasing X, not increasing Y, is the most effective method of increasing Z...*
>
> *The reason for the unexpectedly small effect of ... is uncertain. One possibility is that it was due to...*
>
> *Another possibility is that the method we used ... may have caused smaller increases ...*
>
> *Neither D nor E proved to be effective in causing...*
>
> *Another reason for our lower values could be that...*
>
> *In contrast to previous reports, we found that...*

■ SUMMARY

So, to reduce the pain of writing:

1. Consult and learn from reliable sources on the web, especially those of internationally recognized organizations in your field.

2. Do not try to create a masterpiece of literature or impress with big words; make simplicity and clarity your goals.

3. *Practice makes perfect* (or at least better)—make writing part of your daily routine.

4. Avoid multitasking; when you are writing, focus on that job and do not allow yourself to be distracted by trivial errors or getting things in the wrong order.

5. Learn from what you read, read aloud, and try to manage your time efficiently.

6. Keep an Everyday Book.

CHAPTER 2

WRITING THE FIRST DRAFT

>>>

>>
USE PEN AND PAPER
THE RADMI SEQUENCE
RESULTS AND DISCUSSION—What did you find and what does it mean?
METHODS—How did you do it?
INTRODUCTION—Why did you do it?

>

CHAPTER 2 WRITING THE FIRST DRAFT

What scientists do has never been the subject of a scientific, that is, an ethological[37] *inquiry. It is no use looking to scientific 'papers', for they not only conceal but actively misrepresent the reasoning that goes into the work they describe*[38]

We do not intend to creat poetry or literature and do not care about beauty or elegance here; you want to <u>communicate</u>, to transfer the information that your brain has accumulated, through long experiments and deep thought, into the brains of readers. Can this transfer be improved by beauty and elegance? No! On the contrary, vague, atmospheric language, obscure terms, and other literary strategies essential for setting scenes and transmitting emotional states, are barriers to the clear communication of objective facts.[39] The ultimate goals are to state your evidence and ideas

---

[37] Using scientific methods to study behavior.

[38] Medawar P (1996) *The Strange Case of the Spotted Mice and Other Classic Essays on Science*. Oxford University Press, pages 33-39. Medawar won the Nobel Prize for Physiology and Medicine in 1960 for his work on transplantation. His essays are classics.

[39] Shakespeare, the greatest wordsmith in the English language, made the audience aware of Hamlet's mental state by having him say: *To be, or not to be: that is the question: Whether 'tis nobler in the mind to suffer The slings and arrows of outrageous fortune, Or to take arms against a sea of troubles, And by opposing end them? To die: to sleep; No more; and by a sleep to say we end The heart-ache and the thousand natural shocks That flesh is heir to, 'tis a consummation Devoutly to be wish'd. To die, to sleep; To sleep: perchance to dream: ay, there's the rub; For in that sleep of death what dreams may come When we have shuffled off this mortal coil, Must give us pause: there's the respect That makes calamity of so long life; For who would bear the whips and scorns of time, The oppressor's wrong, the proud man's contumely, The pangs of despised love, the law's delay, The insolence of office and the spurns That patient merit of the unworthy takes, When he himself might his quietus make With a bare bodkin? who would fardels bear, To grunt and sweat under a weary life, But that the dread of something after death, The undiscover'd country from whose bourn No traveller returns, puzzles the will And makes us rather bear those ills we have Than fly to others that we know not of? Thus conscience does make cowards of us all; And thus the native hue of resolution Is sicklied o'er with the pale cast of thought, And enterprises of great pith and moment With this regard their currents turn awry, And lose the name of action.*

The biomedical writer would simply have Hamlet complain: *I am depressed.*

clearly, using simple language, and concisely, without unnecessary words. But, at this stage you just want to get all the necessary information down on the page. Do not allow yourself to be distracted by sequence, grammar, spelling, references, or any other details. Just fill the pages with misspelled words and grammatically incorrect sentences in the order they are generated by your brain.

USE PEN AND PAPER

After a lecture on biomedical writing, a student asked me whether it is better to write with pen and paper or keyboard and screen. Surprised by the question, I tried to think quickly and responded weakly along the lines of preferring pen and paper myself, having learned to write before the invention of word-processors, but that young people like herself might feel more comfortable with keyboard and screen. After thinking about this, I now suggest that using pen and paper is preferable for creative writing, as in the case of a first draft, while keyboard and screen are better for editing and subsequent drafts. In fact, right now I am writing with pen and paper—later I will type this into the document file, probably adding, modifying and deleting material while doing so.

My rationale for preferring pen and paper for the first draft is based on minimizing distractions. We still learn to write with a pen or pencil before learning to use a keyboard. Since using a pen is learned early, this skill is deeply over-learned and requires relatively little brain space, so using a pen is semi-automatic. In contrast, using the QWERTY keyboard is complicated, requiring skill like that of playing the piano—more brain space is needed—and the frequency of typographical errors increases with typing speed. Further distractions are generated by the word-processor itself; red lines indicating spelling errors and green lines suggesting grammatical errors. While these functions are very useful for editing, they are counter-productive when we are trying to focus on writing new material. Also, with a paper notebook and a pen in your bag, you can note down ideas as they occur to you, anytime, anywhere. An electronic notebook needs to be booted up and, sooner or later, connected to a power supply. So, perhaps in the case of writing the first draft, the antique method of pen and paper is better. It is also easier for making marginal notes to yourself for later action, and sketching ideas for graphs and diagrams.

THE RADMI SEQUENCE

While the IMRAD formula describes the sequence in which papers are finally published, manuscripts are rarely, if ever, written in the order Introduction, Methods, Results, and Discussion. This is because few beginning investigators really think deeply about their experiments until they actually write about them. Since the Results occupy your brain at this point, I recommend the RADMI sequence for writing the first draft. This is a more natural way of writing than the artificial separation of Results from Discussion. Write the Results and Discussion together. Write a caption for the figure illustrating result 1, describe result 1 and discuss its meaning, then write a caption for the figure illustrating result 2, describe result 2 and its meaning ... (in the next phase, when editing this draft, the material is cut and pasted into separate sections for Results and Discussion); then the

Methods; and finally, the Introduction. Only after these parts have been completed can you write the Abstract and create an informative Title.

RESULTS AND DISCUSSION
—What did you find and what does it mean?

We do not normally think of the Results, a dense and detailed collection of data, entirely separated from the Discussion, an explanation of what the Results mean. Although some journals sensibly mix Results and Discussion in a more user-friendly way (I am thinking of *Nature* and *Science*, which still publish letters rather than papers), most adhere to the format which insists on the rigorous separation of facts from their meaning. But this does not mean that we must write the Results and Discussion separately in the first draft. When we think about describing a result, it is rational also to think about what that result means.

So, look at your Figure 1. What does it show? Give it a title, usually either a direct statement of the conclusions to be drawn from the figure [such as *Inhibition of dopamine synthesis induces Parkinsonian symptoms* or *X is required for morphogenesis*] or a description of what is being illustrated [such as *Electromyographic patterns during swimming* or *Bisulphate sequencing analysis of DNA methylation*]. Then describe what the reader is looking at—histograms, photomicrographs, typical recordings, scatterplots, Western blots... Draw the reader's attention to what is important in the figure—something increased or decreased, something was absent or present. By now your right hemisphere is creating explanations for these phenomena. Do not ignore it; do not say to yourself, *Leave this until Thursday, when I plan to write the discussion*. Write down your explanation now. Say why you think *A* increased and *B* decreased, why *X* appeared only in *group 4*, why the frequency changed at that particular moment, or why the algorithm generated this unexpected output. Repeat this process for each figure, table, diagram, or other material. It is worthwhile to think of each item as a mini-paper focusing only on what it shows and what that particular data set means. Later, when you begin to edit, it is relatively easy to cut and paste this material into three sections: Figure legends, Results, and Discussion. Furthermore, using this strategy automatically prevents you from repeating details from the figures, and especially from the tables, in the text of the Results. Forcing the reader to struggle through strings of numbers embedded in the text, when these numbers are clearly listed in a table, first is a waste of space (after all, the whole point of a table is to remove the need to describe each value) and second *IT IS UNFAIR TO TORTURE YOUR READERS LIKE THIS*.

METHODS—How did you do it?

Go back to your figures and tables. Describe exactly how you obtained each graph and set of numbers—from the first experiment to the last analysis. Include any ideas related to the limitations of these methods (all methods have limitations).

INTRODUCTION—Why did you do it?

The Introduction to a paper is almost always constructed around a white lie[40]. However, this lie is not only ignored by editors, it is required by the IMRAD formula. If young investigators truthfully answered the question *Why did you do this project?*, the most common answer would make a very brief and uninteresting introduction: *I undertook this project because my supervisor told me to*. Even with experienced and respected investigators, a certain amount of disinformation forms the basis of the introduction. Senior colleagues and friends with whom I have discussed this institutional conspiracy agree that the real reasons behind their work are rarely stated in the paper. Most reasons run along the lines of *I had always wondered if...*; *I had a new student, so I asked him to spend six months on it to see what happened*; *I just thought it would be interesting to...*; or *I just love doing this stuff*. The fact is: no matter what the real reason for starting the project was, you must write down plausible reasons for doing it to justify the time and resources that you used in doing it.

On what previous work was your study based? Look at what you wrote about in the Results and Discussion. Why are they important? What questions do they answer? What hypothesis do they support or refute? Write a justification for doing the experiments, based only on what was known before you started them.

---

[40] A white lie would cause no discord if it were uncovered, and offers some benefit to the liar, the hearer, or both. White lies are often used to avoid offense, such as telling someone that you think that their new outfit looks good, when you actually think that it is a horrible excuse for an outfit. In this case, the lie is told to avoid the harmful realistic implications of the truth. From: http://en.wikipedia.org/wiki/Lie.

■ **EXERCISE**

The living conditions of labourers recruited to work for the French Government during World War I

My use of this photograph deserves some explanation. A big problem in teaching biomedical writing is finding examples that engage the interest of the audience. The life sciences are so wide-ranging that the participants in one workshop may include a worker on proteomics who models protein-drug interactions *in silico*, while next to her is someone who investigates social attitudes towards alternative medicine. Clearly, using a text describing a new algorithm for detecting interaction sites bores the epidemiologist, while a paper revealing the popularity of aromatherapy has the same anesthetic effect on the proteomicist. Furthermore, I found that, no matter what data I used as the basis for a writing exercise, a few workshop members would have special knowledge of the topic and dominate the discussion, while the rest of the group would quietly drift off to sleep. How, then, can the interests of a varied group be satisfied? I needed something that would be of some interest to everyone, but that nobody was likely to be expert at. The answer came one Sunday afternoon as I was relaxing with a newspaper and a beer. This photograph appeared in the newspaper as an example from a collection of negatives found in the attic of a house sold long after the owner's death. Unfortunately, I did not note the source, but assume that since the picture was taken almost a century ago, any copyright has long expired. Using this picture as the basis for a writing exercise with the RADMI formula has proven successful in that it arouses interest, and no workshop participant I have encountered so far has displayed any special knowledge of the living conditions of foreign workers in France during the First World War. The picture contains a lot of information, some of it clear and some of it fuzzy and indistinct. It also only shows part of a room in a building, so it is incomplete. In these ways, the picture is like your data, some definite and some uncertain, while being part of a larger area of study.

Begin by looking at the picture in terms of Results and Discussion. What do you see and what does it mean? Typical responses include:

The photograph shows part of a dormitory with about a dozen beds with blankets and pillows. Four men are looking at the camera. They are young, healthy-looking, but seem bored or unhappy. Three are sitting on beds and one is lying down. They look East Asian and are dressed warmly, so the dormitory is probably cold. Their clothes do not look French, but may be from China or South-east Asia, so these men have not been in France long enough for their clothes to wear out. Three are dressed like farmers, but one is wearing a suit, and has a watch-chain, so he may be from a city. The man closest to the camera is smoking a cigarette, his left hand is on a teapot, and two cups are nearby. There are boxes and tables at the ends of the beds. On shelves above the beds are food bowls, small boxes for personal possessions, and maybe a sheet with photographs from home. The light comes from windows at the far end of the room, so the cameraman did not use a flash. The conditions must be crowded when all the beds are occupied. The picture is depressing.

Now, look at the Methods. How was this picture taken?

A cameraman must have been present; how did he take the picture? Presumably he selected the subjects and the location. If he was French, he probably needed an interpreter to relay instructions to the four men. Did he give the man in the foreground the cigarette? Did he provide the teapot? After arranging his subjects, the cameraman would have to tell them to sit perfectly still until he stopped counting. Since this photograph was taken sometime between 1914 and 1918, the camera probably did not have a shutter and the film was very slow, so a long exposure would be necessary. This part of the method is crucial for interpreting facial expression. If you are asked to smile, and to maintain that smile for ten seconds or more, you find it extremely difficult; a genuine smile is a transient event, the muscles of your face do not usually remain contracted for long. So the easiest option is simply to relax the facial muscles, which produces a neutral expression. Nothing about their emotional state, therefore, can be interpreted from the faces of these men. Whether they are deliriously happy or miserably unhappy, the method ensures that they look neutral. Other questions arise out of thinking about the methods. Were these men selected because they are young and healthy-looking? How did the missing occupants of the other beds look?

Finally, we come to the Introduction. Why was this picture taken?

By this point in the workshop, the participants have usually adopted one of two incompatible hypotheses: (i) that the picture is negative, to be shown in French media as an illustration of how badly foreign workers are treated in France; or (ii) that the picture is positive, to be shown in the Far East as an example of how well foreign workers are treated in France. As the author, it is your job to defend one and criticize the other. We have no time for this now, but we can imagine searching for examples of other photographs from that time, their role in reconstructing historical events, and how photography was used in wartime France and in the Far East. Such background data would contribute to both the Introduction and the Discussion.

Now that we have used the RADMI sequence to brainstorm about the photograph, we have a collection of facts and ideas that need to be organized into a logical sequence to make a story which readers can easily understand. This is attempted in the next chapter.

CHAPTER 2   WRITING THE FIRST DRAFT

■ SUMMARY

When writing a first draft:

1. Use pen and paper.

2. Write in the RADMI sequence.

3. Describe each result and discuss its meaning.

4. Describe each method used to get the results.

5. Outline the background knowledge on which the study was based.

CHAPTER 3

EDITING THE FIRST DRAFT

>>

RESULTS—What did you find?
DISCUSSION—What does it mean?
METHODS—How did you do it?
INTRODUCTION—Why did you do it?
INSTRUCTIONS FOR AUTHORS

>

CHAPTER 3 EDITING THE FIRST DRAFT

I never cease to be amazed by the general inability of physicians, other health professionals, and scientists to communicate in the written word. Their scholarly and creative ideas and insightful data interpretation often seem to get lost in the translation from brain to page. [41]

The first draft was written simply to include everything necessary and without much attention to language and organization; now we must make it clear, concise, and orderly. As the AMA Manual of Style [page 303] says: ... *concise submissions may be given higher priority than long ones (other factors being equal) because they take up a smaller proportion of a journal's resources and total space allotment.*

RESULTS—What did you find?

Read through your combined Results and Discussion and cut all statements that do not directly describe the results; paste them into your new Discussion section. Describe the main findings; do not discuss their meaning. Do not repeat numbers that are already shown in the tables and figures. No matter how complex the tables and figures may be, they should

---

[41] In this way, Catherine D DeAngelis, Editor-in-Chief of the *Journal of the American Medical Association and Archives Journals*, begins the foreword of the 10th edition of the *AMA Manual of Style*. Rather more optimistically, the foreword ends, *Read and understand, write and be understood, and mostly, enjoy.* [Note that the above criticism is mainly directed against native English speakers—most of the contributors to AMA journals are presumably Americans.]

only contain essential information. If the paper is about a method, or if the experiment requires technical skill (as in single neuron recording in awake animals), it is often necessary to show a typical example of the raw data. Then the processed data are shown in tables and figures, with examples of raw data as insets when necessary. If the paper is complex, a summary figure showing the main findings as a schematic diagram or flowchart helps the reader (the description of such a summary figure can be reserved for the Discussion).

■ EXERCISE

Take the Results and Discussion from the exercise in Chapter 2 and delete the parts that express opinions or conclusions and so belong to the Discussion.

The photograph shows part of a dormitory with about a dozen beds with blankets and pillows. Four men are looking at the camera. They are young, healthy-looking, ~~and seem bored or unhappy.~~ Three are sitting on beds and one is lying down. They look East Asian and are dressed warmly, ~~so the dormitory is probably cold. Their clothes do not look French, but may be from China or South-east Asia, so these men have not been in France long enough for their clothes to wear out.~~ Three are dressed like farmers, but one is wearing a suit, and has a watch-chain, ~~so he may be from a city.~~ The man closest to the camera is smoking a cigarette, his left hand is on a teapot, and

CHAPTER 3   EDITING THE FIRST DRAFT

two cups are nearby. There are boxes and tables at the ends of the beds. On shelves above the beds are food bowls, small boxes ~~for personal possessions, and maybe a sheet with photographs from home.~~ The light comes from windows at the far end of the room, ~~so the cameraman did not use a flash. The conditions must be crowded when all the beds are occupied. The picture is depressing.~~

Now, reorganize the statements into logical order. If this were literature, we would probably begin by setting the scene and progressively focusing in; from the general to the particular, from the room to the man in the foreground. But in biomedical fields, we usually begin with the most striking finding and then to more general confirmatory or supporting findings; from the specific to the general. So we begin with the smoking man. [Note that the past tense is used for results.]

The man closest to the camera was smoking a cigarette, his left hand was on a teapot, and two cups were nearby. Four men were looking at the camera. They were young and healthy-looking. Three were sitting on beds and one was lying down. Three were dressed like farmers, but one was wearing a suit, and had a watch-chain. They looked East Asian and were dressed warmly. Boxes and tables were placed at the ends of the beds. On shelves above the beds were food bowls and small boxes. The background showed part of a dormitory with about a dozen beds with blankets and pillows. The light came from windows at the far end of the room,

DISCUSSION—What does it mean?

Summarize the main findings in the same order as described in the Results. Do not begin with a brief introduction to the work; the reader already absorbed this from the Introduction, 15 minutes ago. Relate each finding to the current and relevant literature. Interpret the main findings in relation to the problem or hypothesis raised in the Introduction. Summarize the minor findings and explain how they are consistent or inconsistent with the interpretation of the main result. Include a paragraph of self-criticism. Since no experiment is perfect, point out the limitations. Conclude with a clear and concise re-statement of your results and their importance. Do not repeat that worthless old phrase *Further studies are needed to....* Everybody knows that further studies are needed; that is how science progresses.

■ EXERCISE

As we did for the Results, let us now extract the discussion-related material from the Results and Discussion, Methods, and Introduction of the exercise in Chapter 2. This gives us something like the following:

From Results and Discussion: *The four men seem bored or unhappy. The dormitory is probably cold. Their clothes do not look French, but may be from China or South-east Asia, so these men have not been in France long enough for their clothes to wear out. One may be from a city. Small boxes for personal possessions, and maybe* a sheet with photographs from home are seen. The cameraman did not use a flash. The conditions must be crowded when all the beds are occupied. The picture is depressing.

From Methods: *Presumably the cameraman selected the subjects and the location. If he was French, he probably needed an interpreter to relay instructions to the four men. Did he give the man in the foreground the cigarette? Did he provide the teapot? Because this photo was taken sometime between 1914 and 1918, the camera probably did not have a shutter and the film was very slow, so a long exposure would be necessary. This part of the method is crucial for interpreting facial expression. If you are asked to smile, and maintain that smile for ten seconds or more, you find it extremely difficult; a genuine smile is a transient event, the muscles of your face do not usually remain contracted for long. So the easiest option is simply to relax the facial muscles, which produces a neutral expression. Nothing about their emotional state, therefore, can be interpreted from the faces of these men. Whether they are deliriously happy or miserably unhappy, the method ensures that they look neutral. Other questions arise out of thinking about the methods. Were these men selected because they are young and healthy-looking? How did the absent occupants of the other beds look?*

From Introduction: *By this point in the workshop, the participants have adopted one of two incompatible hypotheses: (i) that the picture is negative, to be shown in French media as an illustration of how badly foreign workers are treated in France; or (ii) that the picture is positive, to be shown in the Far East as an example of how well* foreign workers are treated in France. As the author, it is your job to weigh the evidence and, based on your expertise and experience, defend one, criticize the other, and consider any alternatives. We have no time for this now, but we can imagine searching for examples of other photographs from that time, their role in reconstructing historical events, and how photography was used in wartime France and in the Far East.

This material needs to be organized, which can be done in many ways; we can select a scheme such as:

1. The positive hypothesis
   a. the smoking man
   b. the other men
   c. the surroundings
   d. other ideas
2. The negative hypothesis
3. Self-criticism
4. Conclusion

Using this outline, we get something like this:

Careful examination of the photograph suggests that it was taken to encourage young men in the Far East to work for the French government [1]. This hypothesis is supported by several pieces of evidence. The man in the foreground had a cigarette and tea, suggesting that he had money to spend on small luxuries [1a]. All four men were young, healthy, and appropriately dressed, indicating that they received adequate nourishment, exercise, and clothing [1b].

CHAPTER 3 EDITING THE FIRST DRAFT

Each bed had blankets, and storage space was available [1c]. The possibility that the photographer supplied the cigarette and tea set does not affect our argument. If he did so, this would reinforce the idea that a positive, rather than a negative impression was wanted. Furthermore, only four of at least a dozen beds were occupied. Perhaps the photographer selected the healthiest and best-dressed men for the same reason [1d]. [Further information could be added here after a search through the literature for conditions in the Far East in 1914-1918, such as life expectancy, disease, and the economy, and for documentation on foreign workers in France at that time, such as contracts, pay scales, and mortality.]

On the other hand, it could be argued that the picture was taken to show the poor conditions under which the workers lived. The men did not look happy; none of them was smiling. This may be due to the slow photographic plates used in cameras at that time, requiring long exposures and absolute stillness of the subjects. A natural smile is fleeting and cannot be maintained for long, so the men had to adopt a neutral expression [2].

The major drawback of this study is that it was based on a single photograph. Confirmation or refutation of our hypothesis awaits analysis of other negatives from the same and other sources, and evidence from newspapers, posters, or pamphlets from the Far East that may include such photographs [3].

In conclusion, our analysis suggests that photographs of foreign laborers were used to recruit more of their compatriots to work in France [4].

METHODS—How did you do it?

The crucial factor here is sequence. The general rule is to describe your methods in a rational order: first, you worked on something specific, ranging from an entire ecosystem or population of people to an *in silico* model or a molecule. What were your subjects or molecules and how did you select or obtain them? What procedures did you then carry out, using what equipment, from which suppliers? How did you then analyze the raw data, and what statistical tests did you use?

The importance of sequence was illustrated in an episode from the popular TV show of the 1960s and 1970s, *M * A * S * H*[42]. This comedy series was based on the staff of a Mobile Army Surgical Hospital under wartime conditions. The story in that episode went something like this. A bomb lands in the hospital compound but does not explode. Examination reveals that it was dropped by one of their own aircraft, and listening with a stethoscope tells them that the detonator has not been triggered—no ticking is heard. Quickly getting a copy of the instruction manual, they begin to defuse the bomb. The senior officer, a safe distance away, shouts out the instructions one by one, while two doctors operate on the bomb.

Officer: *Turn nut A ninety degrees clockwise.*

Doctors: *Nut A turned ninety degrees clockwise, OK.*

Officer: *Rotate screw B one hundred eighty degrees counterclockwise.*

Doctors: *Screw B rotated one hundred eighty degrees counterclockwise,*

---

[42] http://www.mash4077.co.uk/index.php.

CHAPTER 3 EDITING THE FIRST DRAFT

OK.

    Officer: *But not before clamping ring C...*

    Doctors: *What*!

    Bomb: *Tick, tick, tick...*

Everyone scatters and the bomb goes off, showering all with pieces of paper carrying a message advising the enemy to surrender. It is a propaganda bomb.

The point for us is that getting methods in the wrong order causes misunderstandings. I recall reading the Methods section of a thesis with increasing alarm. The student described a surgical procedure on rats. As I read through this very long sentence, I began to worry that the thesis would be rejected due to failure to follow the animal care guidelines. With a sigh of relief, I reached the final crucial words ... *after inducing general anesthesia with urethane (1.5 g/kg, i.p.)*. This is something like the *But not before...* of the *M*A*S*H* story. The rat was anesthetized before any surgical procedures were carried out, so the description should begin with *After inducing anesthesia...* or *General anesthesia was induced with...* In another example, the author wrote *After one hour of injection with 5 mg X, we administrated 10 mg Y*. The phrase *After one hour of injection* means the X was continuously injected for 60 minutes. This is not what was done. The author injected X, waited one hour, and then injected Y. The intended meaning is clear with *One hour after injection of 5 mg X, we administered 10 mg Y*. So, when writing your methods, simply set down in words the things you did in the order in which you did them.

Before you even start an experiment, make sure that you have Ethics

Committee approval and informed consent when needed (Declaration of Helsinki[43] or Animal Care Committee[44]) as required by international, national, and institutional regulations, as well as by journals.

Describe your subjects (patients—numbers, inclusion and exclusion criteria; animals—species, strain, number, gender, age and size; sources of tissues, cells, or molecules) and controls.

Outline your protocols—this part should contain enough information, in logical order, for the reader to repeat the experiment (standard procedures need not be described, cite the original work; note deviations from the original work; identify drug and equipment manufacturers by name, city, state and/or country). Provide a diagram of the protocol if necessary, as when the sequence of steps is complicated.

Specify the statistics used and justify their use (especially if they are not standard). Be rigorous about this. Some journals send manuscripts for evaluation of the statistical methods before deciding whether to send them for review, especially in statistics-heavy fields like epidemiology, clinical trials, and computer-based modeling.

■ EXAMPLE

150 male Wistar rats (weight of 190~210 g, age of 6~7 weeks) were divided into three groups at random, test (T) group, experiments (E) group and sham-operation (S) group. The model of injury in kidney of the rat was respectively established in T and E groups,

---

[43] This important document can be downloaded from http://www.wma.net/en/30publications/10policies/b3/index.html.

[44] Internationally recognized guidelines are available at the National Institutes of Health (USA) Office of Animal Care & Use: http://oacu.od.nih.gov/

and 1 *hour of time* was needed. In S *group*, abdomen was opened without injury kidney and all other procedures were same as T and E *groups*. Samples were collected after 6, 12, 24, 48, 72 hours *respectively* in each *group*. The T *group* had injury. Three *groups* had same exposure time. Rat model was prepared according to standard method.[10] Pentothal sodium (40 mg/kg) was injected into biceps femoris 30 minutes before injury. [120 words]

By removing unnecessary words and phrases and changing the sequence, we get:

One hundred fifty male Wistar rats, aged 6-7 weeks and weighing 190-210 g, were randomly assigned to test (T), experimental (E), and sham-operated (S) groups. Thirty minutes after anesthesia with sodium pentothal (40 mg/kg, i. m.), the kidney injury model was created by the standard method [10] in the T and E groups. The same procedures were carried out in the S group, but without kidney injury. Samples were collected from each group 6, 12, 24, 48, and 72 hours later. [80 words]

■ EXERCISE

From the Methods of the exercise in Chapter 2, we are left with:

A cameraman must have been present. After arranging his subjects, the cameraman would have to tell them to sit perfectly still until he stopped counting.

INTRODUCTION—Why did you do it?

The Introduction should <u>not</u> be a review of everything that has been published on the topic since the invention of writing (this is only required for that living fossil of the academic world, the thesis). The work may fill a gap in our knowledge or contribute to resolving a controversy.

Although you often see the main results at the end of the Introduction, this is absolutely unnecessary. The Instructions for Authors in many journals specifically state that this should not be done. Usually, the Introduction should end with a concise statement of the hypothesis to be tested, or the specific aims of the project. Unfortunately, too many editors fail to enforce this policy. From the viewpoint of readers, stating the main results at the end of the Introduction just makes them waste time reading more words. As a reader, I often want to yell at editors and authors: *FIVE MINUTES AGO, I READ THE TITLE, WHICH TOLD ME THE MAIN RESULT. FOUR MINUTES AGO, I READ THE ABSTRACT, WHICH REPEATED THE MAIN RESULT. NOW, YOU WANT TO TELL ME THE MAIN RESULT AGAIN, JUST AS I AM ABOUT TO READ THE RESULTS SECTION! HOW STUPID DO YOU THINK I AM?* At this moment, I would much rather be thinking about what you are trying to persuade me to believe, so I can critically evaluate your results. So, the final paragraph of the Introduction should begin something like: *So, using this new method, we set out to determine whether...* or *Thus, the goal of these experiments was to assess...*

CHAPTER 3   EDITING THE FIRST DRAFT

According to the AMA Manual of Style[45][page 836]:

The introduction should include a concise review of the relevant literature to provide a context for the study question and a rationale for the choice of a particular method. The study hypothesis or purpose should be clearly stated in the last sentence(s) before the "Methods" section. Results or conclusions do not belong in the introduction.

■ EXERCISE

> After removing the materials that were moved to the Discussion, we have:
>
> We have no time for this now, but we can imagine searching for examples of other photographs from that time, their role in reconstructing historical events, and how photography was used in wartime France and in the Far East.

INSTRUCTIONS FOR AUTHORS

(see Appendix I for further details)

Now, it is crucial to read the Instructions for Authors.

If you and your supervisor cannot yet decide which journal your paper will be sent to, a good source of professional advice on manuscript organization is the *Uniform Requirements for Manuscripts Submitted to*

---

[45]   *The AMA Manual of Style: A Guide for Authors and Editors*, 10th Edition (2007), Oxford University Press.

Biomedical Journals: Writing and Editing for Biomedical Publication, produced by the International Committee of Medical Journal Editors[46]. According to their statement of purpose:

The ICMJE created the Uniform Requirements primarily to help authors and editors in their mutual task of creating and distributing accurate, clear, easily accessible reports of biomedical studies. The initial sections address the ethical principles related to the process of evaluating, improving, and publishing manuscripts in biomedical journals and the relationships between editors and authors, peer reviewers, and the media. The latter sections address the more technical aspects of preparing and submitting manuscripts. The ICMJE believes the entire document is relevant to the concerns of both authors and editors.

As soon as you decide which journal your work will be sent to, go to the web site of the journal and carefully read the Instructions for Authors. Some editors are very helpful in telling you exactly what they do want and what they do not want. A fine example was the set of instructions in *Acta Pharmacologica Sinica*[47]. The editor provided clear and direct instructions; here are some examples:

Title:

Words should be chosen carefully for retrieval purposes. All nonfunctional words should be deleted, such as "the", "studies on", "observations of", and "roles of".

---

[46] http://www.icmje.org.

[47] http://www.chinaphar.com/Author-APS.htm. I regret to report that many of the details in this web site changed since I selected these examples. But they are so sensible that I wish to preserve them here.

CHAPTER 3 EDITING THE FIRST DRAFT

Introduction:

The last sentence should state tersely your purpose to do this study (not methods, results, or conclusion).

Results:

Do not write "Tab 1 shows that" or "Fig 2 demonstrated that."

Discussion:

In your conclusion avoid indefinite or ambiguous wording, such as "possible", "perhaps", "maybe", "probably", and "likely". If you are not sure of your conclusion, do more experiments.

Use concise, not redundant, expressions. Examples: after (not following), pig (not porcine), to (not in order to), by (not by means of).

Avoid complicated compound sentences. Delete unnecessary wording, eg, "it has been reported in the past literature that", "as already stated", and "in a real sense".

■ SECOND DRAFT OF EXERCISE

By combining the results of reorganizing our first draft into the IMRAD formula, we have:

INTRODUCTION

Describe examples of other photographs from that time, their role in reconstructing historical events, and how photography was used in wartime France and in the Far East. We therefore set out to analyze this photograph for evidence that it was taken for propaganda purposes.

METHODS

A cameraman was present. After arranging his subjects, the cameraman told them to sit perfectly still until he stopped counting.

RESULTS

The man closest to the camera had a cigarette in his mouth, his left hand was on a teapot, and two cups were nearby. The four men were looking at the camera. They were young and healthy-looking. Three were sitting on beds and one was lying down. Three were dressed like farmers, but one was wearing a suit, and had a watch-chain. They looked East Asian and were dressed warmly. Boxes and tables were placed at the ends of the beds. On shelves above the beds were food bowls and small boxes. The background showed part of a dormitory with about a dozen beds with blankets and pillows. The light came from windows at the far end of the room.

DISCUSSION

Careful examination of the photograph suggests that it was taken to encourage young men in the Far East to work for the French government. This hypothesis is supported by several pieces of evidence. The man in the foreground had a cigarette and tea, suggesting that he had money to spend on small luxuries. All four men were young, healthy, and appropriately dressed, indicating that they received adequate nourishment, exercise, and clothing. Each bed had blankets, and storage space was available. The possibility that the photographer supplied the cigarette and tea set does not affect our argument. If he did so, this would reinforce the idea that a positive, rather than a negative impression was wanted. Furthermore, only four of at least a dozen beds were occupied. Perhaps the photographer selected the healthiest and best-dressed men for the same reason.

CHAPTER 3 EDITING THE FIRST DRAFT

On the other hand, it could be argued that the picture was taken to show the poor conditions under which the workers lived. The men did not look happy; none of them was smiling. This is explained by the slow film used in cameras at that time, requiring long exposures and absolute stillness of the subjects. A natural smile is fleeting and cannot be maintained for long, so the men had to adopt a neutral expression.

The major drawback of this study is that it was based on a single photograph. Confirmation or refutation of our hypothesis awaits analysis of other negatives from the same source, and evidence from newspapers, posters, or pamphlets from the Far East that include such photographs.

In conclusion, our analysis suggests that photographs of foreign laborers were used to recruit more of their compatriots to work in France.

This second draft is not yet ready for submission. It does, however, give us a logical structure to think about and work on. The Introduction can be expanded by including information about the unique value of photographs as historical documents, examples of new data derived from old negatives, and cases of the use of early photography in propaganda. The Methods could be extended by finding out about the most commonly-used cameras in France and the characteristics of the photographic plates used at that time. Further information could be added to the Discussion after a search through the literature for conditions in the Far East in 1914-1918, such as life expectancy, disease, and the economy, and for documentation on foreign workers in France at that time, such as contracts, pay scales, and mortality. As you can see from what I have just written, the exercise provides us with a solid basis from which to construct an interesting and reasonable article. Compare this position with your initial response to the photograph.

■ SUMMARY

1. Reorganize your first draft using the IMRAD formula.
2. Add materials or ideas that arise during the reorganization.
3. Read the *Instructions for Authors* in your target journal.

CHAPTER 4

COMMON ERRORS: ITEMS TO DELETE FROM YOUR FIRST DRAFT AND AVOID FOREVER AFTER

ABBREVIATIONS
ADMINISTRATE
APOSTROPHES
BACK-TRANSLATION
CAN/COULD
COMMON THINGS ARE NOT NECESSARILY POPULAR
DETECTING OR MEASURING?
EQUIPMENTS, RESEARCHES, EVIDENCES
ETC/AND SO ON
EXPENDABLE PHRASES
INCLUDING
NOUN STRINGS
OBSERVED
OBVIOUSLY
OUT-OF-DATE/INAPPROPRIATE TERMINOLOGY
RESPECTIVELY
SENTENCE INVERSION
SIGNIFICANTLY
TENSES
THE PROBLEM OF *THE*
THERE IS...
TILDE (~)
USE IS USEFUL
WITH OR BY?

CHAPTER 4   COMMON ERRORS

When editing, my best friend is the DELETE key[48]

Delete key billboard created by Ji Lee in New York City.

ABBREVIATIONS

Young investigators (YIs) automatically add an abbreviation/acronym (AA) whenever a complex term (CT) or complex sequence of terms (CSOT) appears in the manuscript (MS). However, an AA is only useful if the CT or CSOT is used many times in the subsequent text. Recently, I have noticed AAs being used for terms that never appear again (TTNAAs) in the MS. The usefulness of an AA (UOAA) can be checked by using the

---

[48]   I just made this up.

find function of the word processor (FFWP). **So, YIs should not use TTNAAs and only use AAs for CTs and CSOTs if the UOAA is evident from an FFWP check of the MS.**

I wrote the above as a (slight) exaggeration of the abbreviation reflex. A useful source to check for the generally accepted meaning of any abbreviation or acronym you wish to use is the Biomedical Acronym Database[49]. For example, I checked *MPTP* on that database, and found 79.9% hits for *1-methyl-4-phenyl-1,2,3,6-tetrahydropyridine*, and 3.7% hits for *mitochondrial permeability transition pore*. Therefore, to avoid confusion, the abbreviation for the pore should probably be changed to something else. Many journals discourage the use of abbreviations other than standard ones like *DNA*, *PCR*, or *MRI*. Others limit the number of abbreviations. An extreme form of this sensible hostility to abbreviations is at the *European Journal of General Medicine*[50]:

Abbreviations are permitted, but no more than 3 per manuscript, and then they must be used on every page of the manuscript after they are spelled out (followed by the abbreviation) in both abstract and introduction. Abbreviations are usually limited to terms in the manuscript's title.

ADMINISTRATE

Much to my surprise, my old copy of Webster's Dictionary[51] has a

---

[49] http://invention.swmed.edu/argh/.

[50] http://www.bioline.org.br/info? id = gm&doc = instr.

[51] *Webster's Twentieth Century Dictionary*, Unabridged, Second Edition (1966) The World Publishing Co, Cleveland.

listing for this word, which I have never seen or heard used by any biomedical investigator whose native language is English. Perhaps it is used in business or government documents, in the sense of the administration of a company or department. While it is correct to describe the *administration* of a drug as, for example, intravenous, what you actually do is *administer* it to a patient or animal. You cannot *administrate* a drug.

Delete *administrate* from your vocabulary.

■ EXAMPLE

Rats were <u>administrated</u> of dopamine with intraventricular.

Dopamine was <u>administered</u> to the rats by intraventricular injection.

[Note that these were the specific rats used in the experiments, so a *the* is needed.]

APOSTROPHES

In casual writing, we use apostrophes to indicate missing letters, as in *that's* for *that is*, *hasn't* for *has not*, and *doesn't* for *does not*. This is considered too informal for published papers and ~~shouldn't~~ should not be used.

The apostrophe is also used to indicate possession, as in *the professor's office* or *the student's desk*. Generally, the use of the apostrophe to indicate the possessive case should also be avoided. This strategy also solves the problem of whether to put the apostrophe before the *s*, as in *the patient's symptoms* [one patient], or after it, as in *the patients' symptoms* [many patients]. It is better to say the symptoms of the patient or patients. Exceptions include *according to the manufacturer's instructions*, a phrase that came into common use with the development of reagent kits, and items named after their inventors, such as *Dulbecco's modified Eagle's medium*.

BACK-TRANSLATION

The following examples are the results of back-translation. The English names for many biomedical terms have been given equivalents in Chinese. Because of the difficulty of creating new characters, such terms are usually translated as appropriate combinations of existing characters. The problem arises when an author writes a paper in Chinese and then asks someone, perhaps an English major, to translate it into English. The translator is unlikely to recognize the special meaning of characters representing medical terms and so translates them literally. For example, the three Chinese characters for *immunohistochemistry* are derived from the three components—immunology, histology, and chemistry. The author/translator then re-translated the characters back into English and came up with *immunity organization chemistry*.

You can avoid this problem by checking that the terms you use are common in recent international publications.

CHAPTER 4   COMMON ERRORS

■ EXAMPLES

> *Chose the method of immunity organization chemistry to dye the cell according to the elucidation of the kit.*
>
> Immunohistochemistry was used to stain the cells, according to the instructions with the kit.
>
> [Note that the author appears to have used a Chinese-English dictionary for all three underlined terms.]
>
> *Rabbit resist people antibody*
> Rabbit anti-human antibody
>
> *Manufacture of cells creeping plate*
> Manufacture of cell migration plates
>
> *Twin-coccus is a genus of bacteria found in...*
> Diplococcus is a genus of bacteria found in...

CAN/COULD [when writing about results]

Overuse of these indefinite words may be due to the usual style of expression in the Chinese language. However, in English, *can* and *could* suggest a level of uncertainty, as in *I could meet you for lunch, but I might go to a movie instead.* You almost never want to imply that your results, or the published results of others, are uncertain. So it is strange to say *Acetylcholine can excite mammalian skeletal muscle* (as if acetylcholine had some choice in the matter), when everybody knows that *Acetylcholine excites mammalian skeletal muscle.* So, if your results showed that drug A reduced apoptosis, do not say *we showed that drug A could reduce* apoptosis, be definite about your data and the published data of others. As much as possible, use strong words when describing your results; words like *confirmed*, *demonstrated*, *established*, *revealed*, *showed*, and *verified*.

In the Introduction and Discussion, when you consider alternative hypotheses or interpretations, *can* and *could* are appropriate since real uncertainty exists about alternative hypotheses. When you must speculate, weak words like *imply*, *indicate*, *may*, *might*, *perhaps*, and *suggest*, can be used. But *DO NOT GO TOO FAR*. One weak word near the beginning of the sentence is enough to tell the reader that you are not willing to defend this idea with your life. A sentence containing more than one weak word makes the reader think that this idea is so uncertain that it is not worh considering. For example, *These data suggest that the activity may depend, perhaps, on the interactions between X, Y, and Z. TOO WEAK*! Use of the word *suggest* is an admission that the author is speculating; the rest of the sentence should clearly state what is being suggested: *These data suggest that the activity depends on the interactions between X, Y, and Z.*

■ **EXAMPLES**

In group C, administration of DT can ameliorate disorganization of cytoskeleton in axons (Fig. 2D-F).

In group C, administration of DT reduced the disorganization of the cytoskeleton in axons (Fig. 2D-F).

[Note: since this is describing results, the past tense is used; *ameliorate* is complicated, *reduced* is simple.]

An experiment proved that the PKC activation could induce the synthesis and release of tumor necrosis factor, interleukins, nitric oxide, and so on (reference).

PKC activation induces the synthesis and release of tumor necrosis factor, interleukins, and nitric oxide (reference).

[Note: since this is describing published work, the present tense is used; *prove* is not used much in biomedical writing, since incontrovertible, black-and-white conclusions are rare, so this word is best reserved for mathematical/logical proofs; *and so on* is worthless.]

... almost <u>can</u> be found in all the organs and tissues

... is found in most organs and tissues

[Note: *most* is more concise than *almost all*.]

<u>Researches</u> showed that the drug <u>could</u> eliminate oxygen radicals.

The drug eliminates oxygen radicals.

[Note: since this describes published work, the present tense is used; the plural of *research* is rarely used nowadays.]

... is one kind of multipotent polypeptide, which <u>could</u> inhibit the growth of cells, by inducing apoptosis. X<u>☐</u> <u>could</u> form a complex upon binding to...

... is a multipotent polypeptide, which inhibits cell growth by inducing apoptosis. XII forms a complex on binding to...

[Note: the Chinese-based word-processor used the default font (usually *SimSun*, a Simplified Chinese font) symbol for the Roman numeral *II*. When a font cannot be decoded by English-based word processors it is replaced by an empty box. Always check that your symbols are in standard international font, like *Times New Roman* or *Arial*.]

COMMON THINGS ARE NOT NECESSARILY POPULAR

The word *common* is used mainly to suggest that something occurs often. Mobile phones are common in China. Traveling long distances by train is common in China. The word *popular* contains the meaning of *common*, but adds something more—that the thing is desirable by many people. Having a phone with internet access is popular [many people want one] but not common [too expensive]. Train travel is common, but not as popular as flying. So, you can imagine my surprise when I read statements like: *Nasopharyngeal carcinoma is the most popular form of cancer in southern China* or *Gunshot wounds are much more popular in the USA than in China*. It makes me think that people actually want to contract this dreadful disease or get shot. I speculate that some Chinese-English or English-Chinese dictionary, which is both common and popular, provides both of these words as equivalent to a Chinese character, but I do not know. ㊾

The take-home message is: Use *common*, it is a neutral word; do not use *popular*, which implies the judgment that the thing being described is likable. So, in southern China, nasopharyngeal cancer is both common and extremely unpopular; the same goes for gunshot wounds in the USA.

㊾ I was given this plausible explanation: in an unfortunate translation, two of the three characters in the Chinese term for *Epidemiology*, when used in everyday speech, mean *popular*.

DETECTING OR MEASURING?

When you try to *detect* something, the result can only have one of two values; it is present or it is absent. For example, you may use two-dimensional electrophoresis to *detect* the presence or absence of a protein under different conditions. However, if you then proceed to use densitometry to measure its relative abundance, you are no longer detecting but *measuring, assessing, evaluating, quantifying*... Detection is digital, measurement is analog.

■ EXAMPLES

> *So it is interesting to* detect *subcellular localization of these proteins.*
>
> So it was of interest to determine the subcellular localization of these proteins.
>
> *...full genome microarray was used to* detect *gene expression changes...*
>
> ...full genome microarray was used to quantify the changes in gene expression...
>
> *Fluorescence emission of CFP (470-500 nm) and YFP (526-600 nm) were* detected *before and after bleaching.*
>
> The fluorescent emission of CFP (470-500 nm) and YFP (526-600 nm) was measured before and after bleaching.

[Note that *fluorescence* is a noun and *fluorescent* is its adjective.]

After the histopathological *detection* of grafts...
After the histopathological assessment of grafts...

EQUIPMENTS, RESEARCHES, EVIDENCES

One of the many odd things about English is the fact that some words do not get an *s* added to them when there is more than one. The explanation I found involves the idea of *countability*⑤: a *fact* is a thing that can be counted, so you can have two *facts*; *evidence* is a thing that cannot be counted, so you cannot have two *evidences*; what you have is two *pieces of evidence*. This rule also applies to two *items of equipment* and two *areas of research*. Given the above explanation, it seems that almost nothing is countable in the Chinese language, in that a character meaning something like *item of* is inserted between the number and the thing being described, as in *two items of book* or *seven items of chair*. So, in special cases like *equipment*, English follows the same rule as Chinese.

Equipment, *evidence* and *research* are always singular. Other such words that occur often in biomedical papers are *advice*, *information*, *literature*, *progress* [when used as the plural of the noun *progress*; as a verb it is OK, i. e. *as the disease progresses*], and *work* [as above, *works* works as a verb, as in *the method works*].

---

⑤ http://esl. about. com/od/grammarforbeginners/a/g_cucount. tm.

EXAMPLES

> ...development of novel manufacturing *equipments*...
> ...development of novel manufacturing equipment...
>
> *Previous studies provided evidences that...*
> Previous studies provided evidence that...
>
> *However, still other researches indicate that...*
> However, still other research indicates that...
>
> *We thank Profs. A, B, and C for advices on...*
> We thank Profs. A, B, and C for advice on...
>
> *...have been mentioned in some literatures.*
> ...have been mentioned in the literature [or in some reports].
>
> *With the development of this technique research has made many progresses.*
> With the development of this technique research has made much progress.
>
> *Many works have been made about this problem.*
> Much work has been done on this problem.

ETC/AND SO ON

To me, the use of *et cetera* is the sign of a lazy mind. The writer seems to say, *I can think of a few items, but don't want to make the effort to complete the list. You (the reader) should know them anyway.* If it is important, say, to list the established differential diagnoses in your case, make the list complete. In most biomedical studies, the author wants to select from a list the most important items related to the current study. In this situation, *etc.* is not needed. It is enough to say ... *other factors*, <u>*such as*</u> *a , b , and c , ...* , or ... *underlying mechanisms* , <u>*including*</u> *a , b , and c* ... , or ... *alternative pathways* , <u>*for example*</u> *a , b , or c ....*

Strunk and White[54] say: *In formal writing*, <u>etc.</u> *is a misfit. An item important enough to call for* <u>*etc.*</u> *is probably important enough to be named.*

Never end a partial list with *etc.* or *and so on*, it creates a bad impression.

■ EXAMPLES

> On the other hand, X reduces the amount of antioxidants including glutathione, superoxide dismutase <u>and so on</u>.
>
> On the other hand, X reduces the levels of antioxidants such as glutathione and superoxide dismutase.
>
> These proteins are present in blood, and the main protein of nomal human and animals plasma is AZ, which plays an essential role in modulating cellular signaling in embryonic development, tumorigenesis, angiogenesis <u>and so on</u>.
>
> These proteins are present in blood, and the main protein in normal mammalian plasma is AZ, which plays an essential role in modulating cellular signaling in processes such as embryonic development, tumorigenesis, and angiogenesis.
>
> ... coagulatory factors such as fresh frozen factor, fibrinogen and blood platelet <u>etc.</u>, were used.

---

[54] Strunk W, White EB (2000) *The Elements of Style*. Fourth Edition, Penguin Books, New York, first published in 1913, remains the iconic reference for style in general English writing.

CHAPTER 4 COMMON ERRORS

> ... the coagulatory factors fresh frozen factor, fibrinogen, and platelets were used.
>
> [Note: in this example, these three were the only ones used—they were not part of a longer list of materials.]
>
> ... *inflammation occurs in various organs such as the skin, kidney, intracranium, gastrointestinal tract, genital organs, gallbladder,* <u>*etc*</u>*.*
>
> ... inflammation occurs at various sites, including the skin, kidney, brain, gastrointestinal tract, genitalia, and gallbladder.
>
> [Note: The word *intracranium* is not in my medical dictionary.]

EXPENDABLE PHRASES

The following phrases and many other similar ones, which your right hemisphere likes but just clog up your writing, should be deleted in most cases.

■ <u>EXAMPLES</u>

a total of
as above/below
as already stated
as a matter of fact
as mentioned above/below
as we know
basically

> *further investigations are needed*
>
> *in a word*
>
> *in other words*
>
> *in the present study*
>
> *it has been reported in the literature that*
>
> *it has been well documented that*
>
> *it is of interest to note that*
>
> *it should be noted that*
>
> *it was demonstrated that*
>
> *it was found that*
>
> *we can see that*

INCLUDING

I frequently delete this word but, since it is often used incorrectly by native English speakers, perhaps I no longer need to. Nevertheless, the word *include indicates that what is to follow is only part of a greater whole. To use it when you are describing a totality (as in* 'The 630 job losses include 300 in Redcar and 330 in Port Talbot') *is careless and possibly misleading*[55]. It is misleading in biomedical papers when an author states that *several parameters, including resting membrane potential, peak spike frequency, and acetylcholine release were measured*, when in fact only these three were recorded. The reader expects to find more parameters, but finds none. In

---

[55] Bryson B (2008) *Bryson's Dictionary for Writers and Editors*. Black Swan, London. page 213.

this case, it is more precise to write *the parameters resting membrane potential, peak spike frequency, and acetylcholine release were measured.*

If the list of items is relatively long, just use a colon, as in ... *the pipette solution contained (in mM): 140 CsF, 10 NaCl, 1 EGTA, 10 HEPES, adjusted to pH 7.2 with CsOH (300-310 mOsm/L).* For smaller lists, *comprise* or *consist of* are useful.

■ EXAMPLES

Three networks are used here, including an ABC-MAP, a DEF-MAP, and a network from the GH database.

Three networks were used: an ABC-MAP, a DEF-MAP, and a network from the GH database.

Similar behavior was also found in a number of commercially-available laser diodes, including ABC123, DEF456, and GHI789.

Similar behavior was found in the commercially-available laser diodes ABC123, DEF456, and GHI789.

Thus, ABC processing products including DEF, GHI and JKL were all affected by...

Thus, the ABC processing products DEF, GHI and JKL were all affected by...

Seventy volunteers were recruited, including 30 men and 40 women.

The 70 volunteers consisted of 30 men and 40 women.

Four members of the family, including the proband, her father and two of her father's brothers, provided samples...

> Four members of the family, <u>comprising</u> the proband, her father and two paternal uncles, provided samples...

NOUN STRINGS

By diffusion from the Chinese language, young investigators tend to generate long noun strings (technically, using nouns as modifiers), such as *baseline CD4 cell counts*. Therefore, it is natural for you to use noun strings in your first draft. In the editing phase, you need to add the troublesome little words that are essential in English to make these strings easy to understand: *baseline counts of CD4 cells*. The AMA Manual of Style [p 316] advises *nouns can be used as modifiers, but not more than three*.

■ **EXAMPLES**

> ... *high glucose-induced acute vascular endothelial dysfunction*
> ... *acute induction of vascular endothelial dysfunction by high glucose*
> ... *human fetal cartilage-specific matrix components* ...
> ... *matrix components that are specific to human fetal cartilage* ...
> ... *ischemia-induced acute renal failure*...
> ... *acute renal failure induced by ischemia*...
> ... *oxidative stress-responsive genes*
> ... *genes responsive to oxidative stress*

CHAPTER 4   COMMON ERRORS

> ... *X domain-containing and Y-interacting Z mutant* ...
>
> ... *Z mutant that contains an X domain and interacts with Y* ...
>
> ... *dead recipient heart-kidney transplants...*
>
> ... *recipients of heart-kidney transplants from deceased donors...*
>
> ... *the transcription factor binding sites prediction problem.*
>
> ... *the problem of predicting the binding sites for transcription factors*

OBSERVED

This is an old-fashioned term. It was probably most used in the 19th century, when scientists were *observing* new things through telescopes and microscopes. It is now a vague and passive word, and has generally fallen into disuse. Astrologers *observed* the stars; a biomedical investigator *assesses*, *calculates*, *demonstrates*, *describes*, *detects*, *determines*, *estimates*, *evaluates*, *examines*, *identifies*, *measures*, *notes*, *records*, *shows*—many such active words are available for your use. Of course, if you are describing what you saw while looking down an optical microscope, *observed* is appropriate, but *seen* is simpler and therefore better.

■ EXAMPLES

> *Hypotension <u>seen</u> during induction was <u>observed</u> to be attenuated by...*
>
> *Hypotension during induction was attenuated by...*
>
> [Note that blood pressure can neither be seen nor observed, but it can be measured. The author could have written *The hypotension measured during induction was attenuated by...*]
>
> *Iron overload <u>is observed</u> in chronic liver diseases, such as...*
>
> *Iron overload occurs in chronic liver diseases, such as...*

OBVIOUSLY

According to Webster's Dictionary, *obviously* means: *in an obvious manner*; *evidently, plainly, apparently, manifestly, naturally*. According to me, it means something like: *You would have to be a complete idiot not to see this*, or EVEN A MONKEY COULD WORK THIS OUT. In other words, this is a mildly insulting term to use when describing your work, almost insisting that the reader should agree with you or seem like a fool. I find that nothing in biomedical research is *obvious*. Many words are available to state your assessment more precisely, such as *apparently, clearly, conspicuously, definitively, distinctly, evidently, greatly, markedly, notably, particularly, remarkably, strikingly, surprisingly...* (but never *significantly*, see below). Note that these words are not synonyms; few words of precisely identical meaning occur in English. Always check with a good dictionary to be sure.

CHAPTER 4   COMMON ERRORS

■ EXAMPLES

... but no <u>obvious</u> necrosis at 24-hour; in the group A, mitochondria edema and crista disorder <u>could</u> be seen, which was milder <u>compared with</u> that of the group B. At 12—and 24-hour, there were no <u>obvious</u> changes in the group A [41 words]

... but no necrosis at 24 h. The mitochondrial swelling and disordered cristae were milder in group A than in group B. Group A remained the same at 12 and 24 h. [31 words]

Through studying the value of A group and B group, we can see that there was no <u>significant</u> difference in the pretreatment comparison of two groups ($P > 0.05$); but there was <u>obviously significant</u> difference in the posttreatment comparison of two groups ($P < 0.01$). There was no <u>significant</u> difference in the comparison of posttreatment 24 hours and preoperative in B group ($P > 0.05$), and there was <u>obviously significant</u> difference in the comparison of all the other time of posttreatment and pretreatment ($P < 0.01$) (Tables 1, 2). [81 words]

After reading it once, what does this paragraph tell you about the results? Let us first simplify it by removing *obviously* and *significant*, as well as the P values, since these are included in the Tables:

Through studying the value of A group and B group, we can see that there was no <u>difference in the</u> pretreatment <u>comparison</u> of two groups; but there was <u>difference in the</u> posttreatment <u>comparison</u> of two groups. There was no <u>difference in the comparison</u> of posttreatment 24 hours and preoperative in B group, and there was <u>difference in the comparison</u> of all the other time of posttreatment and pretreatment (Tables 1, 2).

Now, replacing the clumsy *difference in the comparison of* with the simpler *difference between*, we get:

Through studying the value of A group and B group, we can see that <u>there was</u> no pretreatment difference between two groups; but <u>there was</u> posttreatment difference between two groups. There was no difference between posttreatment 24 hours and preoperative in B group, and <u>there was</u> difference between all the other time of posttreatment and pretreatment (Tables 1, 2).

Next, let us get rid of *there was*:

<u>Through studying the value of</u> A group and B group, <u>we can see that</u> no pretreatment difference between two groups; but posttreatment difference between two groups. No difference between posttreatment 24 hours and preoperative in B group, and difference between all the other time of posttreatment and pretreatment (Tables 1, 2).

Finally, we just remove irrelevant words and tidy up the grammar:

Groups A and B did not differ before treatment, but did differ after treatment. Group B at 24 hours after treatment did not change from preoperative values, but did differ at all other post-treatment times (Tables 1, 2). [37 words]

OUT-OF-DATE/INAPPROPRIATE TERMINOLOGY

Especially those of you writing about clinical medicine, please use *Google*(56) (or your favorite search engine) to check that your terminology is up-to-date. Sometimes, ancient terms are retained in a department, because the Chief of Staff learned them from old textbooks translated from one language to another by people without medical experience. For example, I recently encountered the term *hemospasia* in a manuscript; this is an old-fashioned term related to blood-letting or venesection(57).

I have just checked (Google Scholar) several terms for a common (but not popular) disease: *shaking palsy* (3,170 hits, mainly referring to James Parkinson's original paper or other historical topics), *paralysis agitans* (11,000 hits, mainly older papers, and as an alternative to the current name of the disease), and *Parkinson's disease* (353, 000 hits), which is

---

(56) http://www.google.com.

(57) Here is a description of the origin of the term, which I found at: http://www.sil.si.edu/smithsoniancontributions/HistoryTechnology/text/SSHT-0041.txt:

In France, Victor-Theodore Junod (1809-1881) adapted cupping to entire limbs. Shortly after receiving his degree in medicine in 1833, Junod presented at the Academy of Sciences his apparatus, known thereafter as Junod's boot. Junod believed that actual extraction of blood was a dangerous remedy and that the benefits of bleeding might as easily be obtained by his "derivative method," which withdrew blood from the general circulation but allowed it to be returned at will. Junod's boot and Junod's arm, which sold for as much as 25.00 a piece, were constructed of metal and secured against the limb by a silk, and later a rubber, cap. To the boot was attached a flexible tube, stopcock, pump, and if desired, a manometer for measuring the vacuum produced. In chronic illnesses, Junod recommended that the boot be applied for an hour. So much blood was withdrawn from the circulation by use of the apparatus that the patient might easily faint. To explain how his boot worked, Junod invented a theory that he called "hemospasia," meaning the drawing of blood. This was typical of a number of attempts to introduce sophisticated terminology into discussions of traditional remedies. Junod's arm and boot were widely available through American surgical supply companies. As late as 1915, Heinrich Stern, previously mentioned as a latter-day proponent of bloodletting, had no doubt that application of the boot to the foot would relieve congested states of the abdominal viscera.

outperformed by the presently correct *Parkinson disease* (409,000 hits). [It baffles me why neurologists think it is important that diseases named after those who first described them should not carry the *apostrophe S* just because these individuals did not suffer from the disease themselves. Neuroscientists have a lot more to worry about with the nightmarish names of structures in the brain often invented by people on the basis of how they looked; for example, hippocampus (sea horse), thalamus (chamber), substantia nigra (black stuff), amygdala (almond), and my favourite from an investigator who apparently had a sense of humor, substantia innominata (nameless stuff) and on, and on.] You can also use Google, or equivalent, to check the spelling of unfamiliar terms, a procedure I often follow when reading manuscripts on topics that are new to me. For example, typing in *prostagrandin* elicits the response: *About 488 results (0.09 seconds)*; *Did you mean*: *prostaglandin*. Choosing *prostaglandin* gets: *About 682,000 results (0.16 seconds)*. Finally, you can use this trick to decide between apparently equivalent terms, such as epinephrin (6,220 hits), adrenalin (111,000 hits), adrenaline (237,000 hits), and epinephrine (368,000 hits).

■ EXAMPLES

All animals were hemospasiaed through femoral artery each time.

[According to the Applied Medical Research and Development ANH Bulletin[⑧], the term *hemospasia* has been replaced by *acute normovolemic hemodilution*. A *Google* search on 28-Apr-08 gave 799 hits for *hemospasia*, most from non-English or historical sources, and about 15,900 hits for *acute normovolemic hemodilution*. The authors intended to say *All animals were exsanguinated through the femoral artery*.]

---

⑧ http://www.hematicus.com/Bull03.html.

CHAPTER 4 COMMON ERRORS

> ...antibody staining in the endochylema.
>
> ...antibody staining in the cytosol.
>
> [Note that I could not find a definition of *endochylema* in English on the internet; the search led me to a dictionary that gave the definition in Chinese.]

RESPECTIVELY

Webster's Dictionary states: *respectively... with respect to two or more, in the order named or mentioned; as, the first, second, and third prizes went to John, Mary, and George, respectively.*

This is a long and elegant-looking word, so authors may think that using it impresses editors and readers. Its attractiveness to authors (combined perhaps with the inattentiveness of editors) has allowed it to spread through the biomedical literature like a virulent pathogen over the past couple of decades. I always try to follow the advice of Strunk and White[59], who believe that deletion of this word almost always improves any written work. [Their precise comment is: *Respective. Respectively. These words may usually be omitted with advantage.*] This word can only be used correctly in relating two or more lists of linked items, when each list has the same number of items in order: *abcdef* and *123456*, *respectively*, when *a* is linked with *1* and *f* is linked with *6*. The word should never simply be added to the end of a single list of items. If the number of items or the number of

---

[59] Strunk W, White EB (2000) *The Elements of Style.* Fourth Edition, Penguin Books, New York.

83

lists is long, putting them in a table is preferable; this is kind to the reader, who has trouble remembering the items in list 1 while reading the items in list 2. With small numbers of items and lists, describing individual relations (a = 1 , b = 2 , c = 3 , ...) is easier for the reader to absorb.

NEVER USE RESPECTIVELY UNLESS YOU HAVE AN OVERWHELMING NEED TO DO SO (AND EVEN THEN, PLEASE DO NOT USE IT; LET US TRY TO STAMP OUT THIS PANDEMIC, AND SAVE THE LAKES OF INK, FORESTS OF TREES, AND GIGABITS PER SECOND OF BANDWIDTH THAT IT CONSUMES).

■ EXAMPLES

DT was purchased from XYZ pharmaceutical Co. (China), sodium taurocholate and rhodamine conjugated phalloidin were purchased from Sigma Chemical Co. (St Louis, Missouri, America) respectively.

Respectively is redundant here and simply deleting it makes the sentence more concise:

DT was from XYZ Pharmaceutical Co., China; sodium taurocholate and rhodamine-conjugated phalloidin were from Sigma, St Louis, MO, USA.

[Note: no country called America exists; it is a geographical region, like Europe or Asia.]

The animals were killed at 1, 3, 8 hours after the laparatomy by decapitation under Carbon dioxide anesthesia respectively.

Respectively is meaningless here: Under CO_2 anesthesia, the animals were killed by decapitation at 1, 3, or 8 h after the laparatomy.

CHAPTER 4 COMMON ERRORS

Mortality and the mean Apgar scores in two groups were calculated <u>respectively</u>.

[This suggests that the mortality of one group was calculated, and the mean Apgar score of the other group was calculated separately. The author actually means that both values were calculated for both groups. The inclusion of *respectively* creates confusion.]

Mortality and mean Apgar scores were calculated for both groups.

Comparisons of the demographic and tumor characteristics of the two groups of patients with carcinoma, <u>respectively</u>, revealed that ...

[This suggests that that the demographics of one group of patients was compared with the tumor characteristics of the other group of patients. This is not what the author intended. Removal of *respectively* makes the sentence clear.]

Comparisons of the demographic and tumor characteristics of the two groups of patients with carcinoma revealed that ...

The two rats were 7 and 14 days old, respectively.

Rats A and B were 7 and 14 days old, respectively. [This is correct usage, but unnecessary.]

The two rats' respective ages were 7 and 14 days.

The two rats were 7 and 14 days old.

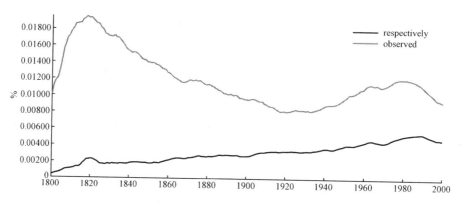

Rate of use of *observed* (upper trace) and *respectively* (lower trace) in books in the Google database between 1800 and 2000[60]. Note that *respectively* has been creeping up from less than once per 1,000 words in 1800 to more than 5 times per 1,000 words in 2000. *Observed*, after a brief recovery in the 1980s, seems to be fading away again.

SENTENCE INVERSION

While writing an essay for an English class, it may be considered elegant to invert the order of events, as in the phrases you have just read, or in *Meanwhile, in the countryside, the air was clear and fresh*. This might score a few more points than *The air was clear and fresh in the countryside*. But in biomedical writing, the reader wants to get to the point immediately, and such stylistic tricks simply make the sentence more difficult for the reader, as in *Meanwhile, prior to calculating the probability density during epoch t_1 with algorithm X, we evaluated the background density at t_{-10}*. In my opinion, lead-in words like *meanwhile* are rarely needed, and writing in the order of events is clearer: *We evaluated the background probability*

---

[60] http://ngrams.googlelabs.com.

density at t_{-10} and then calculated the density at t_1 with algorithm X.

When using general English, it is usual to begin by setting the scene and gradually focusing in on the main event or character, as in the famously awful opening words *It was a dark and stormy night...*[61] But in biomedical writing, we need to get to the point immediately, and leave the details until later, as in *Our main finding was that...* in the Discussion, or *Paradigm A was clearly superior to paradigm B, as shown by...* in the Results, to be followed later by exceptions and details.

■ EXAMPLES

> *At different levels, the pressure was stabilized for 10 min.*
>
> The pressure was stabilized at different levels for 10 min.
>
> *In dopamine release from the striatum, two specific mechanisms have been reported.*
>
> Two specific mechanisms of dopamine release from the striatum have been reported.

SIGNIFICANTLY

My old Webster's Dictionary has no definition for this word in its statistical sense, but authors usually define precisely what they mean by *significantly* in the Methods section as any difference with a *p* value less than

---

[61] The sentence unfortunately continues: *the rain fell in torrents—except at occasional intervals, when it was checked by a violent gust of wind which swept up the streets (for it is in London that our scene lies), rattling along the housetops, and fiercely agitating the scanty flame of the lamps that struggled against the darkness.* From: Lytton EB (1830) *Paul Clifford.* Cassell, New York.

0.05. Having made this clear in the Methods, phrases like *the mean value significantly increased* ($p < 0.05$) or *the mean value did not increase significantly* ($p > 0.05$) are not needed when describing your results. If you feel it is really necessary, add the *p value*, but delete the *significantly*, as in *the mean level increased* ($p < 0.01$), or keep the *significantly* and delete the *p* value. Often, you can omit both when all values are in a table, as in *the concentrations decreased dramatically* (*Table 3*). [My record sighting of this word is a manuscript in which *significantly* was used 27 times. After editing, the word only occurred once, in the Methods section on statistics.]

If you want to emphasize a particular result, many words other than *significantly* are available; for example, *clearly*, *convincingly*, *evidently*, *importantly*, *markedly*, *remarkably*, *substantially*, *surprisingly*, *unexpectedly* ... Note that each of these words is subtly different in meaning, so check with a good dictionary before using one of them.

The AMA Manual of Style [page 888] has this to say about *p* values:

Because the P value represents the result of a statistical test and not the strength of the association or the clinical importance of the result, P values should be referred to simply as statistically significant or not significant; terms such as <u>highly significant</u> and <u>very highly significant</u> should be avoided.

■ EXAMPLE

The serum AB level in normal control group was 60.99 ± 4.25 μmol/L; the levels of CD, EF and GH were 44.88 ± 2.03 pg/ml, 49.00 ± 4.90 U/L and 83.50 ± 25.92 U/L. At 1 hour after treatment, the serum AB levels in each group were <u>significantly</u> lower while CD,

EF and GH were significantly higher than that in normal control group ($P<0.05$); at 1, 3, 24 hour, the levels of AB in group X1,2,3 were significantly higher while CD, EF and GH were significantly lower than in corresponding control groups (Z1,2,3) ($P<0.05$). The levels of AB in group Z2 and Z3 was significantly lower than in group X1 ($P<0.05$), and that in group Z3 was significantly lower than in group Z2 ($P<0.05$). At 1, 3, and 24 hour, the levels of CD, EF, and GH in groups X1,2,3 were significantly lower than in corresponding control groups (Z1,2,3) ($P<0.05$). The levels of CD, EF, and GH in group Z2 were significantly lower than in group Z1 ($P<0.05$), and the levels of CD, EF, and GH in group Z3 were significantly lower than in group Z2 ($P<0.05$) (Tables 1 and 2). [182 words]

Were you able to read through this paragraph once and understand what the main results were? Let us see if we can make this comprehensible. There seem to be three groups: normal control, experimental (X), and corresponding control (Z); three times, 1 (groups X1 and Z1), 3 (groups X2 and Z2) and 24 h (groups X3 and Z3); and four parameters, AB, CD, EF and GH, so the data are complicated. We begin by removing *significantly* and all the numbers, since they are provided in the Tables.

At 1 hour after treatment, the serum AB levels in each group were lower while CD, EF and GH were higher than that in normal control group; at 1, 3, 24 hour, the levels of AB in group X1,2,3 were higher while CD, EF and GH were lower than in corresponding control groups (Z1,2,3). The levels of AB in group Z2 and Z3 was lower than in group X1, and that in group Z3 was lower than in group Z2. At 1, 3, and 24 hour, the levels of CD, EF, and GH in groups X1, 2, 3 were lower than in corresponding control groups (Z1, 2, 3). The levels of CD, EF, and GH in group Z2 were lower than in group Z1, and the levels of CD, EF, and GH in group Z3 were lower than in group Z2 (Tables 1 and 2).

Now, we can try to put this in logical order by time, by copying each statement into a paragraph dealing with 1, 3 or 24 hours. We can remove the redundancies later.

Hour 1: At 1 hour after treatment, the serum AB levels in each group were lower while CD, EF and GH were higher than that in normal control group; at 1, 3, 24 hour, the levels of AB in group X1, 2, 3 were higher while CD, EF and GH were lower than in corresponding control groups (Z1, 2, 3). The levels of AB in group Z2 and Z3 was lower than in group X1. At 1, 3, and 24 hour, the levels of CD, EF, and GH in groups X1, 2, 3 were lower than in corresponding control groups (Z1, 2, 3). The levels of CD, EF, and GH in group Z2 were lower than in group Z1.

Hour 3: At 1, 3, 24 hour, the levels of AB in group X1, 2, 3 were higher while CD, EF and GH were lower than in corresponding control groups (Z1, 2, 3). The levels of AB in group Z2 and Z3 was lower than in group X1. At 1, 3, and 24 hour, the levels of CD, EF, and GH in groups X1, 2, 3 were lower than in corresponding control groups (Z1, 2, 3). The levels of CD, EF, and GH in group Z2 were lower than in group Z1.

Hour 24: at 1, 3, 24 hour, the levels of AB in group X1,2,3 were higher while CD, EF and GH were lower than in corresponding control groups (Z1,2,3). The levels of AB in group Z2 and Z3 was lower than in group X1. At 1, 3, and 24 hour, the levels of CD, EF, and GH in groups X1,2,3 were lower than in corresponding control groups (Z1,2,3).

Now, we can re-write each paragraph without the *1, 2, 3* designations, since they are already determined by whether they are in the paragraph for 1, 3, or 24 hours, and replace the *X* and *Z* designations with easier to read *experimental* and *corresponding control*.

Hour 1: The serum AB levels in the experimental and corresponding control groups were lower while CD, EF and GH were higher than those in the normal control group; the levels of AB in the experimental group were higher while CD, EF and GH were lower than in the corresponding control group. The levels of AB in the corresponding control groups at 3 and 24 h was lower than in group the experimental group. The levels of CD, EF, and GH in groups the experimental group were lower than in corresponding control group. The levels of CD, EF, and GH in the corresponding control group at 3 h were lower than in the corresponding control group.

Hour 3: The levels of AB in the experimental group were higher while CD, EF and GH were lower than in the corresponding control groups. The levels of AB in the corresponding control group was lower than in the experimental group at 1 h. The levels of CD, EF, and

GH in the experimental groups were lower than in corresponding control groups. The levels of CD, EF, and GH in the corresponding control group were lower than in the corresponding control group at 1 h.

Hour 24: The levels of AB in the experimental group were higher while CD, EF and GH were lower than in the corresponding control group. The levels of AB in the corresponding control group was lower than in the experimental group at 1 h. The levels of CD, EF, and GH in the experimental group were lower than in corresponding control group.

After cleaning up a bit, we have:

Hour 1: The serum AB levels in the experimental and corresponding control groups were lower while CD, EF and GH were higher than those in the normal control group. The levels of AB in the experimental group were higher while CD, EF and GH were lower than in the corresponding control group. The levels of AB in the experimental group were higher than those in the corresponding control groups at 3 and 24 h. The levels of CD, EF, and GH in the experimental group were lower than in the corresponding control group. The levels of CD, EF, and GH in the corresponding control group were higher than those in the corresponding control group at 3 h.

Hour 3: The levels of AB in the experimental group were higher while CD, EF and GH were lower than in the corresponding control group. The levels of AB in the corresponding control group were lower than in the experimental group at 1 h. The levels of CD, EF, and GH in the experimental group were lower than in the corresponding control group. The levels of CD, EF, and GH in the corresponding control group were lower than in the corresponding control group at 1 h.

Hour 24: <u>The levels of AB in the experimental group were higher while CD, EF and GH were lower than in the corresponding control group.</u> The levels of AB in the corresponding control group were lower than in the experimental group at 1 h. The levels of CD, EF, and GH in the experimental group were lower than in corresponding control group.

The redundant information is underlined and can be moved to the beginning.

At hours 1, 3 and 24, the levels of AB in the experimental group were higher while CD, EF and GH were lower than in the corresponding control group.

Hour 1: The serum AB levels in the experimental and corresponding control groups were lower while CD, EF and GH were higher than those in the normal control group.

The levels of AB in the experimental group were higher than those in the corresponding control groups at 3 and 24 h.

The levels of CD, EF, and GH in the experimental group were lower than in the corresponding control group. <u>The levels of CD, EF, and GH in the corresponding control group were higher than those in the corresponding control group at 3 h.</u>

Hour 3: <u>The levels of AB in the corresponding control group were lower than in the experimental group at 1 h.</u>

The levels of CD, EF, and GH in the experimental group were lower than in the corresponding control group. <u>The levels of CD, EF,</u>

and GH in the corresponding control group were lower than in the corresponding control group at 1 h.

Hour 24: The levels of AB in the corresponding control group were lower than in the experimental group at 1 h.

The levels of CD, EF, and GH in the experimental group were lower than in corresponding control group.

Now, while the table may show differences between experimental values at one time, and the control values at other times, surely such comparisons are minor or irrelevant. To interpret the data, we must compare like with like, experimental at 3 h with corresponding control at 3 h, not corresponding control at 1 or 24 h. So let us remove this—the reader can see it in the table. If the changes in the corresponding controls are really important, they deserve a separate paragraph.

At hours 1, 3 and 24, the levels of AB in the experimental group were higher while CD, EF and GH were lower than in the corresponding control group.

Hour 1: The serum AB levels in the experimental and corresponding control groups were lower while CD, EF and GH were higher than those in the normal control group.

The levels of CD, EF, and GH in the experimental group were lower than in the corresponding control group.

Hour 3: The levels of CD, EF, and GH in the experimental group were lower than in the corresponding control group.

Hour 24: The levels of CD, EF, and GH in the experimental group were lower than in corresponding control group.

CHAPTER 4　COMMON ERRORS

Next, we just tidy up and remove the redundancy.

Throughout the study, the AB levels were higher and the CD, EF, and GH levels were lower in the experimental groups than in the corresponding control groups. At 1 h, the AB levels were lower and the CD, EF, and GH levels were higher in the experimental and corresponding control groups than in the normal control group. At 3 and 24 h, the CD, EF, and GH levels were lower in the experimental groups than in the corresponding control groups. [80 words]

At last, we have something that tells us what the main results in the table are; but this could still be improved by considering *AB* separately from *CD*, *EF*, and *GH*.

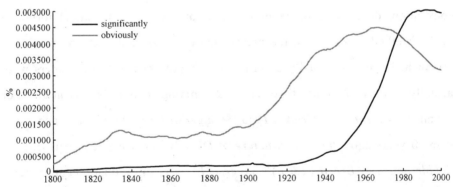

Rate of use of *obviously* (initially upper trace) and *significantly* (initially lower trace) in books in the Google database between 1800 and 2000[62]. Note that *significantly* began to accelerate in the 1930s from less than once per 1,000 words to about 5 times per 1,000 words in 2000. [The paper describing Student's t-test was published in 1908[63].] *Obviously* seems to have peaked in the 1960s.

---

[62]　http://ngrams.googlelab.com.
[63]　Student (1908) The probable error of a mean. *Biometrika* 6(1), 1-125.

TENSES

When you set out to use simple English and short sentences, the verb tense problem is solved by focusing on the present and past. Use the past tense when describing what you actually did. So, the Methods and Results are written in the past tense. Use the present tense when describing work that is published and generally accepted. So, the Introduction is written in the present tense and the Discussion is a mixture of past tense (when referring to your findings) and present tense (when referring to published work). These conventions are widely accepted and useful, especially for the reader, who can use the tense to easily distinguish parts where you describe your results from parts where you relate them to the results of others. Exceptions to these conventions do occur; for example, descriptions of mathematical formulae in the Methods section use the present tense. Also, although the results of established work are usually described in the present tense, the papers were actually published some time ago, so mixing tenses is essential. For example: *Watson and Crick (1953)*[64] *suggested* [past; it happened more than 50 years ago] *that the structure of DNA is* [present; it is still true] *a double helix*; or *Broca (1861)*[65] *suggested* [past; more than a century ago] *that speech is* [present; still accepted] *represented in the left anterior*

---

[64] Watson JD, Crick FHC (1953) A structure for deoxyribose nucleic acid. *Nature* 171, 737-738.

[65] Broca P (1861) Remarks on the Seat of the Faculty of Articulated Language, Following an Observation of Aphemia. *Bulletin de la Société Anatomique*, 6, 330-357. Today, this would be considered a bad title. Something like *A case report of language impairment following left anterior cortical damage* would be better.

CHAPTER 4 COMMON ERRORS

cerebral cortex. If you use these conventions, your writing improves markedly and the pain of writing is reduced. You need never write *will have been* [I forget what tense that is].

THE PROBLEM OF *THE*

The and *a*, and other short words like *at*, *in*, and *with*, are essential for the smooth flow of written English. They are very troublesome, however, because while the native speaker uses them automatically, their equivalents do not exist in the Chinese language[66].

The most useful rule we are all taught in primary school is that *the* is used when something is unique (*the impedance was controlled by...*, *the number of cycles was set to...*), while *a* indicates one of many (*an electrode was placed in...*, *a level-detector was used to...*). This is simple, but not enough for our needs.

An extension of this rule is that a noun often changes from being one of many to being something unique during the writing of a paper. For example, in the Methods it would be correct to describe *an* amplifier from Grass or *a* method of assessing intermolecular distance, since each is one of many. However, later, probably in the Discussion, you may need to refer to these items again. Now, they are unique, because you are referring to the ones you used, as in *when the amplifier was set to...* and *when the method was applied to....* A chair is just a chair, and you are probably sitting in *a* chair

---

[66] Yang JT (1995) *An Outline of Scientific Writing: For Researchers with English as a Foreign Language*. World Scientific Publishing Co. Pte. Ltd, Singapore.

now; but that fact also makes it unique, it is *the* specific chair in which you happen to be sitting.

A further variation on this rule occurs when other words attached to a noun make it special. Some results may have high values, but only one has a value greater than all the others, so it is *the* highest value. Theories are everywhere in the sciences, but the accompanying words identify some as unique; *the* theory of evolution, *the* germ theory, but *a* theory of consciousness, since there are several in competition at present.

A use that apparently contradicts the rules based on uniqueness often appears when writing about the concept of something. When we discuss ideas about central neural functions, for example, we write about *the* brain. Here, we do not mean a specific brain; we do not refer to your brain, my brain, or a mosquito's brain. When we write *the brain*, we mean brains in general. So we write about *the* genome, *the* literature, ...

■ EXAMPLES

Endothelial dysfunction and dendritic cell immune response are early events in atherogenesis.

Here, endothelial dysfunction is a general process, so does not need a *the*. But the immune response of dendritic cells is a specific response, and needs a *the*.

Endothelial dysfunction and <u>the</u> dendritic cell immune response are early events in atherogenesis.

... increased in immunofluorescence test, while nitric oxide release was markedly decreased in nitrite assay.

Both tests are specifically named and so require *the*.

CHAPTER 4   COMMON ERRORS

... increased in <u>the</u> immunofluorescence test, while nitric oxide release was markedly decreased in <u>the</u> nitrite assay.

[Note that *nitric oxide release* could also take a *the*, if a specfic source was referred to, as in ... *while the nitric oxide release from mutated cells...*]

Inhibiting <u>rennin</u>-angiotensin-aldosterone system prevents...

Since the system is specified, a *the* is needed.

Inhibiting the renin-angiotensin-aldosterone system prevents...

[Note that *rennin* is a gastric peptidase, while *renin* is an enzyme of the kidney.]

It was reported that CysLT2 receptor mediates...

The receptor is specified, and *It was reported that* is not needed, since the reference is given at the end of the sentence.

The CysLT2 receptor mediates...

THERE IS...

Beginning a sentence with *There is/are/were...* occurs often in manuscripts I receive. Avoid this construction unless absolutely necessary, because it adds uninformative words.

■ EXAMPLES

> *there is often some restoration of useful function*
> some useful function is often restored
>
> *if there is no suitable donor*
> if no suitable donor is available
>
> *although there is not enough evidence*
> although the evidence is insufficient
>
> *alternatively, there is co-localization of Ca^{2+} channels and vesicles*
> alternatively, Ca^{2+} channels and vesicles are co-localized
>
> *For the patients discharged on the same day as the operation, they were requested to contact the hospital...*
> The patients discharged on the day of operation were asked to contact the hospital...
>
> *For the third experiment, it was added the parameter $\delta\Phi$.*
> The parameter $\delta\Phi$ was added in the third experiment.
>
> *There are issues that need to be resolved.*
> Issues need to be resolved.

TILDE (~)

This squiggle on the upper left key of your keyboard is usually taken to mean *approximately* in English, so *~10* means *about ten* or *approximately* ten. I often see the tilde used to indicate *to* as when *8 ~ 12 μm* is meant to indicate *eight to twelve microns* (this is the common usage in China and several european countries). But to a native English reader, it means *eight approximately twelve microns*, which does not make sense. This use of *to* is indicated by a dash, as in *8—12 μm*.

Only use the tilde to represent *about* or *approximately* [unless you need to use its mathematical meaning of *is equivalent to*; *X ~ Y* in mathematical notation means *X* is equivalent to *Y*].

USE IS USEFUL

Use is a very good word; it is short and its meaning is crystal clear. Why are *utilize*, *employ*, and *adopt* used so much when *used* is perfectly alright? I find it strange to read statements like *Twenty rats were employed in these experiments*. To *employ* suggests payment for doing a job, as in *employer* and *employee*. I wonder how much the investigator paid the rats to participate in the experiments. Similarly, to *adopt* a piece of equipment or technique suggests that it is treated as if it were the author's own child. *Utilize* is just a longer, latin-based (and therefore more aristocratic) way of saying *use*. Technically, nothing is wrong with utilizing, employing, and adopting, but I believe your writing will be clearer, simpler, and therefore better if you use *use*.

WITH OR BY?

Here are a couple of these troublesome little words that infest English but do not have equivalents in Chinese. Were your data collected *with* or *by* a machine or method? An easy way to think of this is to consider whether the data were collected *by* you *with* the help of some device, or were they collected *by* the device itself without you doing anything. For example, if you counted cells under a microscope, the counts were made *with* (the help of) a microscope. If you submitted a protein structure to a database with software that calculated matching probabilities, the results were generated *by* the software.

■ **EXAMPLES**

> *After the treatment by 6-BA or UTB...*
> After treatment with 6-BA or UTB...
> [Note: the patient was treated by the doctor with a drug.]
> *... the specific cleavage of ABC with DEF3 and GHI9...*
> ... the specific cleavage of DEF3 and GHI9 by ABC...
> [Note: in the original form, the reader could not tell which was cleaving what. It was only by further reading to understand the context did it become clear that ABC was cleaving DEF3 and GHI9.]

CHAPTER 5

POTENTIAL DANGERS: ETHICS AND PLAGIARISM

ETHICS
PLAGIARISM

CHAPTER 5   POTENTIAL DANGERS: ETHICS AND PLAGIARISM

To know what is right and not to do it shows a lack of courage[67]

Two major areas of moral and legal concern arise when one wishes to publish biomedical work in an international journal: the ethical use of experimental materials, including animals and humans, and plagiarism.

ETHICS

First, the editor must be satisfied that any living material or component derived from a live source that you used in experiments was obtained and treated in an appropriate, lawful, and humane manner. These materials may range from populations of human beings (as in an epidemiological survey) down to the level of single genes or molecules. Academic institutions are expected to have appointed Ethics Committees, whose job is to ensure that proposed projects conform to internationally-agreed ethical guidelines before any research is begun. Make sure that your research proposal is approved by your Ethics Committee before you start any work. The rights of patients and volunteers, and the responsibilities of researchers working with people, are set out in the *Declaration of Helsinki: Recommendations guiding physicians in biomedical research involving human subjects*[68], a document that is occasionally reviewed and updated by the international community.

For example, the *Instructions for Authors* of *Medical Care* state:

---

[67]   Confucius (~496-406 BC).
[68]   http://www.wma.net/e/policy/b3.htm.

It is the author's responsibility to ensure that a patient's anonymity is carefully protected and to verify that any experimental investigation with human subjects reported in the manuscript was performed with informed consent (where required) and followed all the guidelines for experimental investigation with human subjects required by the institution(s) with which all the authors are affiliated. Please document whether the study was approved by an Institutional Review Board. Authors should mask patients' eyes and remove patients' names from figures unless they obtain written consent from the patients and submit written consent with the manuscript. ⑩

In the case of animal studies, the instructions in *Cell Metabolism* require:

All experiments on live vertebrates or higher invertebrates must be performed in accordance with relevant institutional and national guidelines and regulations. In the manuscript, a statement identifying the committee approving the experiments and confirming that all experiments conform to the relevant regulatory standards must be included in the Experimental Procedures section. The Editors reserve the right to seek comments from reviewers or additional information from authors on any cases in which concerns arise. ⑦

A comprehensive and detailed set of guidelines covering the use of experimental animals and human subjects and the responsibilities of authors, reviewers, and editors is free to download from the *Society for Neuroscience* site. ⑪ Check the society of your own discipline for this kind of information.

---

⑩ http://edmgr.ovid.com/mdc/accounts/ifauth.htm.
⑦ http://www.cell.com/cell-metabolism/authors.
⑪ http://www.sfn.org/skins/main/pdf/Guidelines/ResponsibleConduct.pdf.

CHAPTER 5 POTENTIAL DANGERS: ETHICS AND PLAGIARISM

Ignorance of or disregard for the ethical issues surrounding your particular area of research leads to great difficulties. Here is one of the many examples regularly reported in *Science* and *Nature* (while most of us aspire to be published in these journals, this is not the best way to do it):

from *Science* Vol. 302, page 1657, 5 December 2003:

A cautionary tail. Immunologist Chen Dong has a message for his fellow researchers: When in doubt, check with your Institutional Animal Care and Use Committee (IACUC). The University of Washington (UW), Seattle, has barred Dong from conducting animal research for at least a year after the committee documented an array of violations, including cutting the tips off mouse tails (for tissue analyses) without proper anesthesia. Dong, 36, who came to UW 3 years ago, has also had to retract a recent high-profile paper from the Journal of Clinical Investigation because the IACUC hadn't fully approved the study.

A contrite Dong says his inexperience led to the potentially career-ending missteps, and that he plans to repeat and resubmit the retracted results. And he's relieved that his studies will be able to continue under the watchful eye of colleague Andrew Farr, who has been given temporary oversight of animal work in Chen's 12-person lab. "I regret that I didn't understand how things worked," he says. "And I strongly recommend that everyone work closely with [the] IACUC."

GET APPROVAL FROM THE APPROPRIATE COMMITTEE BEFORE YOU BEGIN ANY EXPERIMENTS.

PLAGIARISM

The other major ethical concern is not specific to biomedical research, but we have to address the problem of plagiarism, and especially learn how to avoid this type of fraud. This strange-looking word comes from the Latin *plagiare*, to kidnap or abduct, along with *plagiarius*, which means kidnapper, seducer, plunderer.

If I write that plagiarism is the unacknowledged use, as one's own, of the work of another person, whether or not such work has been published, then I am guilty of plagiarism. I am guilty because I make you think that these are my words. But in fact I took them from a published source without telling you—I kidnapped them. However, if I write that plagiarism is "... the unacknowledged use, as one's own, of the work of another person, whether or not such work has been published" [From the Graduate Handbook 2004-2005, University of Hong Kong, page 65], I am not guilty of plagiarism because I indicate the copied material with quotation marks, and identify the source. [Note that this definition specifies *whether or not such work has been published* to include copying from essays or take-home exams submitted by classmates.]

The following statements are from the AMA Manual of Style (pages 157-158):

Plagiarism is the appropriation of another person's ideas, processes, results, or words without giving appropriate credit.

CHAPTER 5　POTENTIAL DANGERS: ETHICS AND PLAGIARISM

Four common kinds of plagiarism are listed:

1. Direct: Verbatim[72] *lifting of passages without enclosing the borrowed material in quotation marks and crediting the original author.*

2. Mosaic: *Borrowing the ideas and opinions from an original source and a few verbatim words or phrases without crediting the original author. In this case, the plagiarist intertwines his or her own ideas and opinions with those of the original author, creating a "confused, plagiarized mass".*

3. Paraphrase: *Restating a phrase or passage, providing the same meaning but in a different form without attribution to the original author.*

4. Insufficient acknowledgement: *Noting the original source of only part of what is borrowed or failing to cite the source material in a way that allows the reader to know what is original and what is borrowed.*

An excellent booklet by David Gardner, *Plagiarism and How to Avoid It*, is available at the web site of the Centre for Applied English Studies[73] at the University of Hong Kong.

With the wide availability of information on the web, and the *cut-and-paste* function in word-processors, plagiarism has become a major problem among undergraduate and postgraduate students (and principal investigators) in universities world-wide. To combat this problem, many companies have developed plagiarism-detecting software (e. g. *Turnitin*[74]), which allows universities and publishers to automatically scan essays, theses, and manuscripts for evidence of plagiarism. By comparing the contents of a

---

[72]　Word-for-word.
[73]　http://caes.hku.hk/plagiarism/
[74]　http://turnitin.com/staic/index.html.

paper with huge databases of published material, copying is easily detected and the genuine source identified. *Turnitin* is used at the University of Hong Kong, and I have recently learned that Universities in Mainland China (including Zhejiang University) are introducing a Chinese language-based version of such software (TMLC⑦⑤) to scan manuscripts such as postgraduate theses for plagiarized content. The publishers of international journals are also beginning to subject submitted manuscripts to scanning for *identical or paraphrased chunks of text that appear in previously published articles* and *one journal reported rejecting 23% of accepted submissions after checking for plagiarism.*⑦⑥

Be especially careful to avoid *patchwriting*, a method that some of my students and colleagues told me they used when beginning to write. The following was taken from a report in *Science*, Vol. 324, page 1005, 22 May 2009:

*Many apparent instances of plagiarism picked up by Déjà vu*⑦⑦ *reflect a strategy known as "patchwriting"—an underrecognized problem in scientific publishing... Patchwriters lift large portions of the introduction, scientific design, and other sections of a published paper, then plug in details from their own experiment. "They don't take the data, but they take the scientific design," says Beth Notzon, who has taught classes on publication ethics to young physicians at M. D. Anderson Cancer Center in Houston, Texas, ...*

---

⑦⑤ http://check2.cnki.net/tmlc, developed by China National Knowledge Infrastructure (http://www.global.cnki.net).

⑦⑥ Butler D (2010) Journals step up plagiarism policing: Cut-and-paste culture tackled by CrossCheck software. *Nature* 466, 167 (5 July).

⑦⑦ Déjà vu is a database of duplicate publication in the scientific literature at http://spore.swmed.edu/dejavu/

CHAPTER 5 POTENTIAL DANGERS: ETHICS AND PLAGIARISM

"They're able to repeat the whole thing but in a different population of patients."

The article continues with a detailed description of the trouble that followed when an author in Mainland China copied more than 95% of a paper published by someone else, simply changing the focus from one type of cancer to another and plugging in his own results. In the end, the paper was retracted.

Furthermore, Notzon stated that *She was startled to find that many foreign scholars at M. D. Anderson, particularly those from Asia, consider it* [patchwriting] *perfectly appropriate.* "We had a young woman visiting from China who taught writing and editing in China, and she said laughingly, 'Oh, we encourage this sort of thing because people don't have good idiomatic English.'" But, Notzon says, patchwriting is "wrong because it's really a kind of plagiarism—they're taking someone else's research idea."

DO NOT PLAGIARIZE; IT WILL DESTROY YOUR CAREER!

CHAPTER 6

OTHER THINGS

>> >

>>

ABSTRACT
ACKNOWLEDGEMENTS
COVER LETTER
FIGURE LEGENDS (CAPTIONS)
KEYWORDS
NAMES
REFERENCES
THESIS/DISSERTATION
TITLE
WORD PROCESSORS: Chinese *versus* English

>

CHAPTER 6   OTHER THINGS

The devil is in the details[78]

ABSTRACT

Young investigators tend to underestimate the extraordinary importance of the Abstract. Your first few publications are likely to be abstracts in the proceedings of conferences. They therefore provide potential employers with direct evidence about your suitability for a job. *DO NOT TREAT ABSTRACTS LIGHTLY; THEY STAY WITH YOU FOREVER.*

Briefly answer <u>ALL FOUR</u> IMRAD questions: Why you did the study, how you did the study, what you found, and what the findings mean. Limit the results to the main finding. Obey the restrictions in the Instructions to Authors. Often, the questions of why and how the project was done are answered in one sentence, e. g. *To determine whether... we measured...* Examples of excellent abstracts are easily found in *Nature* and *Science*.

■ EXAMPLE[79]

> During cell division, mitotic spindles are assembled by microtubule-based motor proteins[1,2]. The bipolar organization of spindles is essential for proper segregation of chromosomes, and requires plus-end-directed homotetrameric motor proteins of the widely conserved

---

[78] This means that *Even the grandest project depends on the success of the smallest components.* http://www.bartleby.com/59/3/devilisinthe.html.

[79] From the instruction for authors in *Nature*, at http://www.nature.com/nature/authors/gta.

kinesin-5 (BimC) family[3]. Hypotheses for bipolar spindle formation include the 'push—pull mitotic muscle' model, in which kinesin-5 and opposing motor proteins act between overlapping microtubules[2,4,5]. However, the precise roles of kinesin-5 during this process are unknown. Here we show that the vertebrate kinesin-5 Eg5 drives the sliding of microtubules depending on their relative orientation. We found in controlled in vitro assays that Eg5 has the remarkable capability of simultaneously moving at ~ 20 nm s^{-1} towards the plus-ends of each of the two microtubules it crosslinks. For anti-parallel microtubules, this results in relative sliding at ~ 40 nm s^{-1}, comparable to spindle pole separation rates in vivo[6]. Furthermore, we found that Eg5 can tether microtubule plus-ends, suggesting an additional microtubule-binding mode for Eg5. Our results demonstrate how members of the kinesin-5 family are likely to function in mitosis, pushing apart interpolar microtubules as well as recruiting microtubules into bundles that are subsequently polarized by relative sliding. We anticipate our assay to be a starting point for more sophisticated in vitro models of mitotic spindles. For example, the individual and combined action of multiple mitotic motors could be tested, including minus-end-directed motors opposing Eg5 motility. Furthermore, Eg5 inhibition is a major target of anti-cancer drug development, and a well-defined and quantitative assay for motor function will be relevant for such developments. [253 words]

  The first three sentences (*During... microtubules*) provide the background and sentence four (*However... unknown*) states the problem;

CHAPTER 6 OTHER THINGS

sentences five to eight (*Here... Eg5*) describe the results; and the remaining sentences discuss the significance of the work.

ACKNOWLEDGEMENTS

Provide the official name of the funding agency, grant number, and the name(s) of the author(s) holding the grant. After obtaining their consent, thank people who gave technical support, provided materials, commented on the manuscript, or provided other help.

Nature suggests that:

Acknowledgements should be brief, and should not include thanks to anonymous referees and editors, inessential words, or effusive comments. A person can be thanked for assistance, not "excellent" assistance, or for comments, not "insightful" comments, for example. Acknowledgements can contain grant and contribution numbers[80].

COVER LETTER

Often, a simple statement is enough:

Dear Professor X,

Please find attached a copy of our manuscript entitled "..." by "..."

---

[80] http://www.nature.com/nature/authors/gta/index.html.

which we submit for possible publication in "...".

Yours sincerely,

Sometimes, the Instructions for Authors require statements specifying such things as conflict of interest[81], or that you have not previously published any of the material. For example, the *Author Guidelines* of *PLoS Biology* state:

Authors are asked at submission to declare whether they have any financial, personal, or professional interests that could be construed to have influenced their paper. [82]

Also, some journals may ask for an explanation of why you think your paper should be published there; this may consist of an abstract, with additional statements about the originality and importance of the work. For example, the *Information for Authors* in *Cell* states:

Each submission should be accompanied by a cover letter, which should contain a brief explanation of what was previously known, the conceptual advance provided by the findings, and the significance of the findings to a broad readership. A cover letter may contain suggestions for appropriate reviewers and up to three requests for reviewer exclusions. The cover letter is confidential to the editor and will not be seen by reviewers. [83]

PLoS Biology[84] gives precise instructions about what should be in the

---

[81] Such as receiving financial support from the company that manufactures the drug that you investigated.
[82] http://journals.plos.org/plosbiology/guidelines.php.
[83] http://www.cell.com/authors.
[84] http://www.plosbiology.org/static/guidelines.action.

cover letter:

Please include a cover letter of no more than 600 words that provides brief answers to the following questions:
What is the scientific question you are addressing?
What is the key finding that answers this question?
What is the nature of the evidence you provide in support of your conclusion?
What are the three most recently published papers that are relevant to this question?
What significance do your results have for the field?
What significance do your results have for the broader community (of biologists and/or the public)?
What other novel findings do you present?
Is there additional information that we should take into account?
You may also include in the cover letter requests to exclude specific scientists from the evaluation process. Please provide a reason for doing so. Please also read our policy about competing interests before submitting your inquiry.

It is a good idea to consult the journal's mission statement, which should tell you what kinds of research it publishes, before writing this covering letter. Always consult the *Instructions for Authors* to be sure.

FIGURE LEGENDS (CAPTIONS)

Each figure with its caption is like a tiny paper, informative on its own without the reader having to refer to the text to understand it. So it needs a title that describes the general intent of the figure, as in *Fig. 1. Dynamic range of temperature-sensitive cells in...* [The language in captions tends to be somewhat telegraphic, omitting *the* and *a* except where necessary.] Then each component is described. In the case of a simple graph, the axes are identified and that is enough: *Plot of firing rate (Hz) against temperature (°C)*. In complex figures with illustrations and histograms, each component is dealt with: *A. Photomicrograph of...* ; *B. Histogram showing averaged data from...* ; *C. Schematic diagram of...* ALL abbreviations and items that appear in the figure must be included in the caption. If an abbreviation or other item is not needed, remove it. Cluttered figures containing unexplained items are bad figures.

KEYWORDS

Select keywords from among the Medical Subject Headings (MeSH), which is updated weekly by the National Library of Medicine (National institutes of Health, USA).⑧⑤ Well-chosen keywords are essential for people searching the web for papers on a specific topic. You want the appropriate readers to find your paper easily. Do not make up your own keywords.

---

⑧⑤ http://www.nlm.nih.gov/mesh/meshhome.html.

CHAPTER 6 OTHER THINGS

■ EXAMPLE

Using the MeSH browser to search for keywords related to the term *proteomics*, I found a list beginning:

Albumins

Algal Proteins

Amphibian Proteins

Amyloid

Antifreeze Proteins

Apoproteins

Aprotinin

Archaeal Proteins

Armadillo Domain Proteins

Avian Proteins

and ending:

Serpins

Silk

Silver Proteins

Thioredoxins

Thymosin

Tissue Inhibitor of Metalloproteinases

Transcription Factors

Ubiquitinated Proteins

Ubiquitins

Viral Proteins

NAMES

The editors of international journals can be confused by Chinese names, especially those with just two characters, such as *Ma Xin* or *Jia Shen*. You can help the editors simply by capitalizing your family name, as in *MA Xin* or *Jia SHEN*. Furthermore, if you have the more usual three-character name, it is better to spell the forenames separately or hyphenate them, as in *RU Xiao Chen* or RU *Xiao-Chen*; this makes it easier for readers to find your papers since your name is listed as *XC Ru* (rather than *X Ru*, which would result if you used the form *RU Xiaochen*; this would generate more false-positives in a search).

REFERENCES

References are sources of information (standard values, methods, databases, reviews), support (compatible data or interpretations), and opposition (incompatible data or interpretations), to help the reader understand the relevance of your work. They are used to provide sources of further details, to form the basis of a hypothesis, to support or refute an argument, and to give credit to the work of others.

See the *Instructions for Authors*. Follow the required format consistently. Two main citation styles are used by biomedical journals,

CHAPTER 6 OTHER THINGS

either numbered in order of appearance in the manuscript as in *Nature*[86], or alphabetically by first author and date as in the *EMBO Journal*.[87] Variations occur in the details, so you need to consult the *Instructions for Authors* of your target journal.

Only cite a reference if you have read it. An investigator may misinterpret another's work, thus introduce an error into the literature, and such an error can proliferate through the literature if the original source is rarely consulted. IF YOU HAVE NOT READ THE PAPER, DO NOT CITE IT.

Commercially available software such as *Reference Manager*[88] and *EndNote*[89] are useful for maintaining your bibliography and have the feature of automatically converting references to the most common journal formats.

■ EXAMPLES

Vancouver format

Nature:

1. Varki, A. & Altheide, T. Comparing the human and chimpanzee genomes: searching for needles in a haystack. *Genome Res.* **15**, 1746-1758 (2005)

2. Bustamante, C. D. *et al.* Natural selection on protein-coding genes in the human genome. *Nature* **437**, 1153-1157 (2005)

3. Khaitovich, P. *et al.* Parallel patterns of evolution in the genomes and transcriptomes of humans and chimpanzees. *Science* **309**, 1850-1854 (2005)

---

[86] *Nature* Guide to Authors: http://www.nature.com/nature/authors/gta/index.html.
[87] The *EMBO Journal* Guide For Authors: http://www.nature.com/emboj/guide_for_authors.html.
[88] http://www.refman.com/
[89] http://www.endnote.com/

Science:

1. C. E. Finch, M. C. Pike, M. Witten, Slow mortality rate accelerations during aging in some animals approximate that of humans. *Science* **249**, 902 (1990).

2. R. E. Ricklefs, Life-history connections to rates of aging in terrestrial vertebrates. *Proc. Natl. Acad. Sci. U.S.A.* **107**, 10314 (2010).

3. C. Finch, *Longevity, Senescence and the Genome* (Univ. of Chicago Press, Chicago, 1990).

Proceedings of the National Academy of Sciences:

1. Pener MP, Simpson SJ (2009) Locust phase polyphenism: An update. *Adv Insect Physiol* 36:1-272.

2. Uvarov B (1966) *Grasshopper and Locusts* (Cambridge Univ. Press, 5 Cambridge), Vol 1.

3. Enserink M (2004) Can the war on locusts be won? *Science* 306:1880-1882.

Harvard format

Journal of Neuroscience:

Aonurm-Helm A, Berezin V, Bock E, Zharkovsky A (2010) NCAM-mimetic, FGL peptide, restores disrupted fibroblast growth factor receptor (FGFR) phosphorylation and FGFR mediated signaling in neural cell adhesion molecule (NCAM)-deficient mice. *Brain Res* **1309**:1-8

Bodrikov V, Leshchyns'ka I, Sytnyk V, Overvoorde J, den Hertog J, Schachner M (2005) RPTPalpha is essential for NCAM-mediated p59fyn activation and neurite elongation. *J Cell Biol* **168**:127-139.

Brennaman LH, Maness PF (2008) Developmental regulation of

GABAergic interneuron branching and synaptic development in the prefrontal cortex by soluble neural cell adhesion molecule. *Mol Cell Neurosci* **37**:781-793.

The EMBO Journal:

Abbas T, Dutta A (2009) p21 in cancer: intricate networks and multiple activities. *Nat Rev Cancer* **9**: 400-414

Ambros V (2004) The functions of animal microRNAs. *Nature* **431**: 350-355

Aoi T, Yae K, Nakagawa M, Ichisaka T, Okita K, Takahashi K, Chiba T, Yamanaka S (2008) Generation of pluripotent stem cells from adult mouse liver and stomach cells. *Science* **321**: 699-702

Molecular and Cellular Neuroscience:

D. Cai, J. Qiu, Z. Cao, M. McAtee, B. S. Bregman and M. T. Filbin, Neuronal cyclic AMP controls the developmental loss in ability of axons to regenerate, *J. Neurosci.* **21** (2001), pp. 4731-4739.

J. K. Chilton, Molecular mechanisms of axon guidance, *Dev. Biol.* **292** (2006), pp. 13-24.

B. J. Dickson, Molecular mechanisms of axon guidance, *Science* **298** (2002), pp. 1959-1964.

More than you are ever likely to want to know about citations is available at www.ncbi.nlm.nih.gov/books/NBK7256, where you can download for free 26 chapters, 7 appendices, and updates dealing with the topic[90]

---

[90] Patras K, Wendling D (Eds) (2007) *Citing Medicine*, 2nd Edition. *The NLM Style Guide for Authors, Editors, & Publishers.* National Library of Medicine, National Institute of Health, Bethesda.

(including how to cite e-mails, audiocassettes, photographs, and newspaper articles).

THESIS/DISSERTATION

I learned from a thesis about dissertations[91] that students were first required to write them before the end of the 18th century in German universities. In my opinion (and I am not alone in this), the thesis in its present form is a huge waste of time. In this I have the support of W. Malcolm Reid[92], who raised five objections to the dissertation: (i) it is not a useful tool in scientific communication, (ii) the writing skills in thesis writing are not those required for publication, (iii) its length has become excessive and discouraging, (iv) it has no standard format, and (v) when unpublished, it represents a failure in the training system for PhDs. As a teacher of writing for publication, I am particularly angry about the second objection. I find that I have to help doctoral students to *UNLEARN* the writing skills they developed while writing a thesis. For example: the thesis must be as long as possible, while the manuscript must be concise; the thesis must contain every little thing the candidate did, while the manuscript must contain only novel and important findings; the thesis introduction must reference everything published in the topic since the invention of writing, while the manuscript introduction should contain only enough information for

---

[91] Barton MD (2005) Dissertations: Past, present, & future. *Theses & Dissertations*, Paper 2777. http://scholarcommons.usf.edu/etd/2777.

[92] Reid WM (1978) Commentary: Will the future generations of biologists write a dissertation? *BioScience* 28 (10), 651-654.

the reader to understand why the project was done. [I just looked at my own doctoral dissertation and found that it contains 161 pages. When rewritten in publishable form, the resulting paper was 12 pages long.]

I therefore again agree with Reid on the solution to this problem. A modern thesis should consist of three sections at most: (i) a literature review showing that the candidate has read and understood the literature (this is usually not intended for publication, but is needed to satisfy university requirements; it might be replaced by a research proposal if one was required at the beginning of the program), (ii) *Production of one or more acceptable journal-style manuscripts, which will contribute to the advancement of knowledge, should constitute the major ... requirement*[92] (i. e., usually about 30-40 double-spaced pages, including figures and references), and (iii) if necessary, an appendix or appendices containing additional but as yet incomplete or unsatisfactory information (this could be useful for future data-mining by the candidate or the supervisor).

Although Reid and others before and since have reasonably suggested easing this ancient burden imposed on our postgraduate students, historical and academic inertia has prevailed generally, but not everywhere. I still have hope.

TITLE

State the main finding or your message to the reader. Often, we see titles that do not tell us as much as they could; for example *Effect of X on the development of Y in patients with anemia*. The word *effect* is not informative. It is better to say *X delays (or accelerates, inhibits, prevents...*) *the development of Y in patients with anemia.*

Avoid vague terms[93]—*Aspects of...* [I confess that the title of my first publication, my honours thesis at Aberdeen University, began with the words *Aspects of the neuromuscular physiology of...*], *Effects of..., Factors involved in..., New features of..., Some properties of..., A study of...,* or *X modulates* or *influences* or *alters Y*. Use direct language. See the *Instructions for Authors* for the layout of the title page.

■ EXAMPLES

> Five titles listed in the Citation Classics[94] for 1993:
>
> Thymidine incorporation as a measure of heterotrophic bacterioplankton production in marine surface waters: evaluation and field results.
>
> An algorithm for the machine calculation of complex Fourier series.
>
> Nucleotide sequence of human monocyte interleukin 1 precursor cDNA.
>
> Experimental nephrotic syndrome induced in rats by aminonucleoside. Renal lesions and body electrolyte composition.
>
> Insulin stimulates the phosphorylation of the 95,000 dalton subunit of its own receptor.

---

[93] While unsuccessfully searching the internet for examples of bad titles, I found that the latest James Bond movie has the incomprehensible title *Quantum of Solace*; to me, this is like saying *kilogram of anger* or *centimeter of disappointment*. Consult your dictionary—I challenge you to make sense of it.

[94] http://garfield.library.upenn.edu/classics1993/classics1993.html.

CHAPTER 6 OTHER THINGS

WORD PROCESSORS: Chinese *versus* English

I am typing this manuscript with *Times New Roman* font because it is used world-wide and preferred by most international journals. Also, I am using the 12-point font size because it is easy to read. Unfortunately, most Chinese language word processors use *SimSun* and *10.5-point* as defaults. *SimSun* font looks like this. I am unable to show you 10.5-point because this size is not available on my (English language) word processor. So, when your final draft is ready, click *Edit* and *Select All*, then click *Times New Roman* and *12* in the font boxes. If this is successful, all is well. If the font boxes remain blank, you have a problem, since something in your manuscript is not in this format, probably symbols.

Symbols such as °C, μ, α, Σ... probably appear somewhere in your manuscript. A problem arises when symbols in *SimSun* (or other Chinese language fonts like *PMingLiu*) are not recognized by English language word processors, which replace each one with an empty box. So when you type $-80\,°C$, the reviewer reads $-80\,\square$, or when you write *50* μm, the reader sees *50* $\square$*m*, which causes confusion. So, when you use the *Insert Symbol* function, make sure that you change the font from the default to *Times New Roman* before searching for the symbol you need. A good example is *degrees Celsius*. In *SimSun*, it is a single symbol which looks like this: ℃. In Times New Roman, a specific symbol is used for degrees, and looks like this: °. Then the letter C is added to give °C.

The most strange and frustrating example occurred when I was running the spell-checker on a manuscript and it insisted that *findings* and *fluorescence* were mis-spelled but I could not see anything wrong with them. Further checking showed that any word with the letters *f* and *i* or *f* and *l* together was tagged as incorrectly spelled. By magnifying the font, I could see that these were not pairs of letters but actually single characters. Then a search through the symbols chart identified them as *fl* (latin small ligature FL) and *fi* (latin small ligature FI). In the world of typography, a ligature is two or more letters combined into one character, as for the *a* and *e* in *orthopædics* or *pædiatrics* in English English (such things are generally ignored in American English). [I have so far failed to persuade the principal investigator to ban the use of ligatures, and so have to deal with them each time a new manuscript is sent to me.]

It is worth the effort to go through you manuscript once more to ensure that the symbols are correct. This will avoid irritating the reviewer and help to increase the probability that your manuscript will be accepted.

Times New Roman font in Microsoft Word.

CHAPTER 6 OTHER THINGS

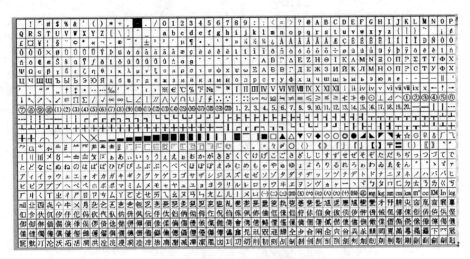

SimSun font in Microsoft Word.

FINAL WORDS

FINAL WORDS

About a century ago, two heroic attempts were made to standardize written English. Fowler opens his book, *The King's English*[95], by writing:

Any one who wishes to become a good writer should endeavour, before he allows himself to be tempted by the more showy qualities, to be direct, simple, brief, vigorous, and lucid.

Similarly, Quiller-Couch in his *On the Art of Writing*[96] says about Style:

Whenever you feel an impulse to perpetrate a piece of exceptionally fine writing, obey it—whole-heartedly—and delete it before sending it to press. Murder your darlings.

So, KEEP IT SIMPLE. After you have mastered the skill of simple, clear writing, then you can think of making your style more elegant, if you feel the need.

SEEK CRITICISM at all stages in your writing. This is the only way to detect errors in logic, sentences that are difficult to understand, and questions that are not addressed. When we write about our own work, we tend to develop a selective blindness, especially to those parts we are not sure about. Give your material to classmates, teachers, colleagues, or friends, and ask them to point out the parts that are not clear. Even after all these years, I dare not submit a piece of work until it has been read by several others. When your study is published, treat your informal editors to a meal, and offer to do the same work for them.

---

[95] Fowler HW (1909) *The King's English*, 2nd ed. Available at www.bartleby.com/116/101.html.
[96] Quiller-Couch A (1916) *On the Art of Writing*. Available at www.bartleby.com/190/12.html.

I hope you have enjoyed reading this book more than I did writing it (I did enjoy writing much of it, but some parts gave me a headache). I also hope that, by now, you are writing with at least some enthusiasm every day, and will soon experience the special joy of seeing your name in print.

Finally, although I have tried to include all the important topics and minimize the errors, I have undoubtedly left out some crucial items and failed to detect mistakes. Dear reader, if (when) you detect omissions and errors, please send your comments to me, so that I can continue to improve.

APPENDIX I SELECTED ADVICE FROM *INSTRUCTIONS FOR AUTHORS*

A link which provides the instructions to authors for over 6,000 journals in the health and life sciences is at The University of Toledo (*http://mulford.meduohio.edu/instr/*).

1. GENERAL

1.1 *Nature*[97] instructions for authors include the following helpful comments:

How to write a scientific paper

A number of articles and websites provide detailed guidelines and advice about writing and submitting scientific papers. Some suggested sources are:

SciDev.Net's Practical guides section[98]

...

The classic book Elements of Style *by William J. Strunk, Jr (Humphrey, New York, 1918) is now published by Bartleby.com (New*

---

[97] http://www.nature.com/authors/author_resources/how_write.html.
[98] http://www.scidev.net/en/practical-guides/how-do-i-write-a-scientific-paper-.html.

York, *1999*) *and is freely available on the web in searchable format*[19].

Advice about how to write a Nature journal paper is provided in the Nature Physics Editorial Elements of style[20].

Dr Leslie Sage, a senior Nature editor, has written an article 'Writing a clear and engaging paper' in Astronomy Communication, 290, 221 (Springer, 2003), which is freely available at Nautilus, for personal use only[21].

Dr. Sage states: *I am often asked if papers authored by people for whom English is not their first language are at a disadvantage in the peer review process. The emphatic answer is "no"—it is exceedingly rare that an author's weak grasp of English is relevant to either referees' assessments of the science or to an editorial decision. In fact, two of the worst written papers I have seen in my time at Nature came from native-English speakers based at a major UK university.*

...

Researchers whose first language is not English often find it useful to either ask a colleague whose native language is English to review the manuscript before submission to a journal, or to use one of the many services that will, for a fee, edit papers to ensure the English is clear and well written. One such service is Nature Publishing Group Language Editing[22].

---

[19] http://www.ebook3000.com/The-Elements-of-Style-Fourth-Edition_42798.html.
[20] http://www.nature.com/nphys/journal/v3/n9/full/nphys724.html.
[21] http://blogs.nature.com/nautilus/2008/04/post_26.html.
[22] http://languageediting.nature.com/

APPENDIX I SELECTED ADVICE FROM *INSTRUCTIONS FOR AUTHORS*

1.2   *Virology*[103] is concise; note that results should neither appear in the introduction nor be repeated in the discussion:

Introduction: State the objectives of the work and provide an adequate background, avoiding a detailed literature survey or a summary of the results.

Results: Results should be clear and concise.

Discussion: This should explore the significance of the results of the work, not repeat them. A combined Results and Discussion section is often appropriate. Avoid extensive citations and discussion of published literature.

Material and methods: Materials and methods should provide sufficient information to permit the work to be repeated and should be kept concise by referring to previously published procedures. With increasing studies on pathogenicity of viruses, it is important that the provenance of viruses be stated clearly.

Conclusions: The main conclusions of the study may be presented in a short Conclusions section, which may stand alone or form a subsection of a Discussion or Results and Discussion section.

1.3   *PNAS*[104] does not allow you to boast about doing something new or being the first to do something:

Text. Describe procedures in sufficient detail so that the work can be repeated. Methods must be presented after Results and Discussion. Follow the spelling and usage given in Webster's Third New International Dictionary or the Random House Dictionary of the English Language. Avoid laboratory

---

[103] http://www.elsevier.com/wps/find/journaldescription.cws_home/622952/authorinstructions.
[104] http://www.pnas.org/site/misc/iforc.shtml.

jargon. Correct chemical names should be given, and strains of organisms should be specified. Trade names should be identified by an initial capital letter with the remainder of the name lowercase. Names of suppliers of uncommon reagents or instruments should be provided. Use Système International (SI) units and symbols whenever possible. <u>Statements of novelty and priority are not permitted in the text.</u>

1.4 *Plant Physiology*[05] does not permit boasting, nor does it publish work that just reports new findings; the experiments must test hypotheses:

Because the methodology of plant science has come to encompass everything from biochemistry and chemistry to immunochemistry and microscopy, from structural biology to molecular biology, from genetics to live cell imaging, submissions are welcome regardless of experimental approach. Accepted papers must either present novel findings and uncover new biological meaning and/or significance of the process, or use novel and useful approaches that will enable scientific progress. <u>*The Journal will not publish papers that contain purely descriptive information, that are merely confirmatory, or that are preliminary reports of partially completed or incompletely documented research findings of uncertain significance, or reports documenting well-known processes in a species in which this process has not yet been documented.*</u> *Papers that report the purification of proteins, the cloning of genes, isolation of new mutants, or microarray/Affymetrix data must address hypotheses about functional aspects of plants. Plant Physiology will accept profiling data papers* <u>*only when they test a scientific hypothesis and are biologically significant.*</u> *Papers should be concise and*

---

[05] http://www.plantphysiol.org/site/misc/ifora.xhtml

avoid unnecessary redundancy, especially in the Discussion section. Statements of priority or first finding are generally not permitted in Plant Physiology.

2. ENGLISH ENGLISH *versus* AMERICAN ENGLISH

The quotation *England and America are two countries separated by a common language* is attributed to the (Irish) dramatist George Bernard Shaw. Although amusing, it does not make much sense to me, having lived and worked in both countries, as well as in Canada, where both versions are generally recognized. No sense of *separation* based on language is evident (although other cultural differences are proudly maintained).

Nevertheless, some editors are very particular about the version of spelling used (especially the editors of UK journals). The *Journal of Neuroendocrinology*[09] provides this useful summary of the major differences in spelling (English to the left, American to the right):

Spelling
Manuscripts should be written in English, in accordance with the Oxford English Dictionary. Examples of rules include:

    ise not ize (eg characterise, visualise, anaesthetise, luteinising)
    ae not e (eg anaesthetic, anaemic, chimaera)
    oe not e (eg oestrogen, oestradiol, dioestrous, pro-oestrus)
    double L (eg signalling, labelled)
    re not er (eg fibre, microtitre, centre, metre)
    our not or (eg behaviour, colour)

---

[09] http://www.wiley.com/bw/submit.asp?ref=0953-8194.

oph not ope (eg somatotroph, gonadotrophin)

gogue not gog (eg secretagogue, analogue)

ph not f (eg sulphate)

mme not m (eg programme)

neurone not neuron

grey not gray

[Note: To his or her credit, this editor has a sense of humor, stating: The purpose of writing is to convey information and ideas from one mind to another. Good writing achieves this efficiently, whether the subject is sex or science, and even if, as is often the case in neuroendocrinology, the subject is both.]

So, before submitting your final draft (drapht? draught?), consult the Instructions for Authors, set your spell-checker to English (United Kingdom) or English (United States), and run a final scan.

3. EQUATIONS

Make sure you express mathematical notation as required by the journal.

3.1 For example, the *Journal of Experimental Medicine*[①] prefers:

Do not use the Word 2007 Microsoft default math editor since it contains incompatibilities that prevent us from using equations created with this editor.

Please use the Design Science Equation Editor (formerly the default Word editor) or MathType rather than the new default math editor featured

---

① http://jem.rupress.org/site/misc/ifora.xhtml.

in the Insert ribbon. To use either Equation Editor or MathType, in the Insert ribbon, click "Object" and choose object type "Microsoft Equation 3.0" or "MathType Equation". The Equation Editor toolbar or MathType window will appear and will work as in previous versions of Word.

3.2 PLoS Biology[⑩] states:

If you are using Word 2007 and your manuscript will contain equations, you must follow the instructions below to make sure that your equations will be editable when you save the file as a Word 2003 document. PLoS cannot accept articles containing equations that are not editable in Word 2003.

You can ensure that your equations remain editable in Word 2003 by enabling "Compatibility Mode" before you begin. To do this:

Open a new document.

Save as "Word 97-2003 Document (*.doc)."

Several features of Word 2007 will now be inactive, including the built-in equation editing tool. You can now insert equations in one of two ways:

Go to Insert > Object > Microsoft Equation 3.0 and create the equation.

Use MathType to create the equation. MathType is the recommended method for creating equations.

If, when saving your final document, you see a message saying "Equations will be converted to images". This means that your equations are no longer editable and PLoS will not unable to accept your file.

NOTE: If you have already composed your article in Word 2007 and

---

[⑩] http://www.plosbiology.org/static/guidelines.action.

used its built-in equation editing tool, your equations will become images when the file is saved down to Word 97-2003. You will need to edit your document and insert the equations using one of the two ways specified above.

4. METHODS

4.1 *The New England Journal of Medicine*[09] on statistical methods:

The basis for these guidelines is described in Bailar JC III, Mosteller F. Guidelines for statistical reporting in articles for medical journals: amplifications and explanations. Ann Intern Med 1988;108:266-73.

Exact methods should be used as extensively as possible in the analysis of categorical data. For analysis of measurements, nonparametric methods should be used to compare groups when the distribution of the dependent variable is not normal.

Results should be presented with only as much precision as is of scientific value. For example, measures of association, such as odds ratios, should ordinarily be reported to two significant digits.

Measures of uncertainty, such as confidence intervals, should be used consistently, including in figures that present aggregated results.

Except when one-sided tests are required by study design, such as in noninferiority trials, all reported P values should be two-sided. In general, P values larger than 0.01 should be reported to two decimal places, those between 0.01 and 0.001 to three decimal places; P values smaller than 0.001 should be reported as $P < 0.001$. Notable exceptions to this policy include P values arising in the application of stopping rules to the analysis of

---

[09] http://www.nejm.org/page/author-center/manuscript-submission.

APPENDIX I   SELECTED ADVICE FROM *INSTRUCTIONS FOR AUTHORS*

clinical trials and genetic-screening studies.

In manuscripts that report on randomized clinical trials, authors may provide a flow diagram in CONSORT format and all of the information required by the CONSORT checklist. When restrictions on length prevent the inclusion of some of this information in the manuscript, it may be provided in a separate document submitted with the manuscript. The CONSORT statement, checklist, and flow diagram are available on the CONSORT website.

4.2   *Blood*[10] is concerned about image manipulation:

(This set of instructions is adapted with permission from the Journal of Cell Biology instructions to authors.)

Note that <u>no specific feature within an image may be enhanced, obscured, moved, removed, or introduced</u>. If groupings of images from different parts of the same gel or microscopic field, or from different gels, fields, or exposures are used, they must be made explicit by the arrangement of the figure (i.e., by inserting black dividing lines) and in the text of the figure legend, explaining what steps were taken to produce the final image and for what reason. Adjustments of brightness, contrast, or color balance are acceptable if they are applied to the whole image and as long as they do not obscure, eliminate, or misrepresent any information present in the original, including backgrounds. Without background information, it is not possible to evaluate how much of the original gel is actually shown. Nonlinear adjustments (e.g., changes to gamma settings) must be

---

[10]   http://bloodjournal.hematologylibrary.org/site/authors/authorguide.xhtml#organization.

disclosed in the figure legend. *The use of special software tools (e. g. , erasing, cloning) available in popular image-editing software is strongly discouraged* unless absolutely necessary, and any such manipulations must be explained in the figure legend.

All images in Figures and Supplemental information from manuscripts accepted for publication are examined for any indication of improper manipulation or editing. Questions raised by *Blood* staff will be referred to the Editors, who may then request the original data from the authors for comparison with the submitted figures. Such manuscripts will be put on hold and will not be prepublished in *Blood* First Edition until the matter is satisfactorily resolved. If the original data cannot be produced, the acceptance of the manuscript may be revoked.

Cases of deliberate misrepresentation of data will result in revocation of acceptance and will be reported to the corresponding author's home institution or funding agency.

5. LANGUAGE

5.1 *Molecular and Cellular Proteomics*[⑪] has this advice for authors whose first language is not English:

Authors who are not native English speakers may seek assistance with grammar, vocabulary, and style when submitting papers to MCP to help maximize the accuracy and impact of the journal submission, as well as aid in communicating ideas to fellow scientists and reviewers. Several companies provide revising, editing, and proofreading services for scientific and

---

⑪ http://www.mcponline.org/site/misc/itoa.xhtml.

APPENDIX I SELECTED ADVICE FROM *INSTRUCTIONS FOR AUTHORS*

medical research documents. These include:

http://www.bioedit.co.uk

www.biosciencewriters.com

www.bostonbioedit.com

www.sciencedocs.com

www.bioscienceeditingsolutions.com

Please note that neither the MCP nor ASBMB has used these services and thus cannot attest to the quality of their work.

5.2 *Journal of Zoology*[⑫] is concise and allows abstracts to be published in languages other than English:

Abstract of not more than 300 words which should list the main results and conclusions. The abstract should also explain the importance of the paper in a way that is accessible to non-specialists. <u>Authors may submit non-English abstracts for online publication to allow the international research community greater access to published articles.</u> Translated abstracts should be submitted in pdf format as supplementary material. The Editors have no input into the content of supplementary material, therefore accuracy is the sole responsibility of the authors.

Keywords. A maximum of eight keywords may be suggested.

Introduction, which should not provide a review of the area of work but should introduce the reader to the aims and context for the work described.

Materials and Methods should be sufficient to allow the work to be

---

⑫ http://onlinelibrary.wiley.com/journal/10.1111/(ISSN)1469-7998/homepage/ForAuthors.html.

replicated, but should not repeat information described fully elsewhere.

Results should be restricted to a factual account of the findings obtained and the text must not duplicate information given in Tables and Figures.

Discussion. This should point out the significance of the results in relation to the reasons for undertaking the research.

5.3 *PLoS Biology*[13] accepts translations in the author's first language as supporting information:

Although we encourage submissions from around the globe, we require that manuscripts be submitted in English. As a step towards overcoming language barriers, we encourage authors fluent in other languages to provide copies of their full articles or abstracts in other languages. Translations should be submitted as supporting information and listed, together with other supporting information files, at the end of the article text.

5.4 *Journal of Pharmacology and Experimental Therapeutics*[14] recommends capitalized initial letters for trade names of drugs:

Generic drug names are used in text, tables and figures. Trade names may be given in parentheses following the first text reference, but should not appear in titles, figures, or tables. <u>*Whereas trade names are capitalized, generic or chemical names are not.*</u> *The chemical structure of new compounds (or a citation to the published structure) must be given. The form used in calculating concentrations (e. g., base or salt) must be indicated.*

---

[13] http://www.plosbiology.org/static/guidelines.action.

[14] http://jpet.aspetjournals.org/site/misc/ifora.xhtml.

APPENDIX I SELECTED ADVICE FROM *INSTRUCTIONS FOR AUTHORS*

6. LEGAL ISSUES

6. 1   The *International Committee of Medical Journal Editors*[15] provides a standard form for the disclosure of potential conflicts of interest and includes the following advice:

This section asks about your financial relationships with entities in the bio-medical arena that could be perceived to influence, or that give the appearance of potentially influencing, what you wrote in the submitted work. You should disclose interactions with ANY entity that could be considered broadly relevant to the work. For example, if your article is about testing an epidermal growth factor receptor (EGFR) antagonist in lung cancer, you should report all associations with entities pursuing diagnostic or therapeutic strategies in cancer in general, not just in the area of EGFR or lung cancer.

Report all sources of revenue paid (or promised to be paid) directly to you or your institution on your behalf over the 36 months prior to submission of the work. This should include all monies from sources with relevance to the submitted work, not just monies from the entity that sponsored the research. Please note that your interactions with the work's sponsor that are outside the submitted work should also be listed here. If there is any question, it is usually better to disclose a relationship than not to do so.

For grants you have received for work outside the submitted work, you should disclose support ONLY from entities that could be perceived to be affected financially by the published work, such as drug companies, or

---

[15]   http://www.icmje.org/coi_disclosure.pdf.

foundations supported by entities that could be perceived to have a financial stake in the outcome. Public funding sources, such as government agencies, charitable foundations or academic institutions, need not be disclosed. For example, if a government agency sponsored a study in which you have been involved and drugs were provided by a pharmaceutical company, you need only list the pharmaceutical company.

Copyright is the exclusive legal right to reproduce, publish, and sell written intellectual property.

Before your paper is published, the journal usually requires you to sign over the copyright to the publisher.

6.2　For example, the instructions for authors in *Metabolomics*[16] state:

It is the policy of Springer to own the copyright of all contributions it publishes. To comply with U. S. Copyright Law, authors are required to sign a copyright transfer form before publication. This form returns to authors and their employers full rights to reuse their material for their own purposes. Authors must submit a signed copy of this form with their manuscript.

6.3　*The Lancet*[17] is more demanding:

Authors will be asked to sign a transfer of copyright agreement, which recognises the common interest that both journal and author(s) have in the protection of copyright. We accept that some authors (eg, government employees in some countries) are unable to transfer copyright. However,

---

[16] http://www.springer.com/life + sciences/biochemistry + %26 + biophysics/journal/11306.

[17] http://www.thelancet.com/lancet-information-for-authors/after-publication.

APPENDIX I   SELECTED ADVICE FROM *INSTRUCTIONS FOR AUTHORS*

such open-access policies do not provide anyone other than The Lancet the right to make in any form facsimile copies of the version printed. All requests to reproduce or make available anything in the journal—in whole or in part, in electronic or in any other form, including translation—must be sent to...

APPENDIX II TOP JOURNALS

The five top-ranked journals by impact factor (2010) from the selected subject categories (excluding reviews) are:

Anatomy & Morphology:

Brain Structure & Function (4.982)

Developmental Dynamics (3.018)

Journal of Anatomy (2.410)

Cells Tissues Organs (2.302)

Zoomorphology (1.800)

Behavioural Sciences:

Behavioral & Brain Sciences (21.592)

Trends in Cognitive Science (9.686)

Cortex (7.251)

Advances in the Study of Behavior (5.870)

Genes Brain & Behavior (4.345)

Biochemistry & Molecular Biology:

Cell (32.401)

Nature Medicine (27.887)

Nature Chemical Biology (15.808)

Molecular Psychiatry（15.470）

Molecular Cell（14.194）

Biology：

PLoS Biology（12.469）

FASEB Journal（6.515）

Philosophical Transactions of the Royal Society B（6.053）

Chronobiology International（5.576）

Bioscience（5.510）

Cell Biology：

Cell（32.401）

Cancer Cell（26.925）

Cell Stem Cell（25.943）

Nature Medicine（25.430）

Nature Cell Biology（19.407）

Computer Science，Interdisciplinary Applications：

Medical Image Analysis（4.248）

Journal of Chemical Information & Modeling（3.822）

IEEE Transactions on Medical Imaging（3.545）

Journal of Computer-Aided Molecular Design（3.374）

MATCH-Communications in Mathematical & in Computer Chemistry（3.291）

Engineering，Biomedical：

Biomaterials（7.882）

Acta Biomaterialia（4.822）

Medical Image Analysis（4.248）

IEEE Transactions on Medical Imaging (3.545)

Journal of Tissue Engineering & Regenerative Medicine (3.543)

Environmental Sciences:

Energy & Environmental Science (9.446)

Frontiers in Ecology & the Environment (8.820)

Global Change Biology (6.346)

Environmental Health Perspectives (6.087)

Global Biochemical Cycles (5.263)

Genetics & Heredity:

Nature Genetics (36.377)

Trends in Ecology & Evolution (14.448)

Genome Research (13.588)

Genes & Development (12.889)

American Journal of Human Genetics (11.680)

Infectious Diseases:

Lancet Infectious Diseases (16.144)

Clinical Infectious Diseases (8.186)

Emerging Infectious Diseases (6.859)

AIDS (6.348)

Journal of Infectious Diseases (6.288)

Medicine, Research & Experimental:

Nature Medicine (25.430)

Journal of Experimental Medicine (14.776)

Journal of Clinical Investigation (14.152)

Molecular Aspects of Medicine (10.552)

Trends in Molecular Medicine(10.308)

Microbiology：

Cell Host & Microbe（13.728）

PLoS Pathogens（9.079）

Advances in Microbial Physiology（8.556）

Clinical Infectious Diseases（8.186）

Current Opinion in Microbiology（7.714）

Nanoscience & Nanotechnology：

Nature Nanotechnology（30.306）

Nano Letters（12.186）

Nano Today（11.750）

Advanced Materials（10.875）

ACS Nano（9.855）

Neurosciences：

Behavioral & Brain Sciences（21.952）

Molecular Psychiatry（15.470）

Nature Neuroscience（14.191）

Neuron（14.027）

Trends in Neuroscience（13.320）

Oncology：

CA-A Cancer Journal for Physicians（94.262）

Cancer Cell（26.925）

Journal of Clinical Oncology（18.970）

Lancet Oncology（17.764）

Journal of the National Cancer Institute（14.697）

Pharmacology & Pharmacy:

Drug Resistance Updates (12.312)

Trends in Pharmacological Sciences (11.050)

Pharmacology & Therapeutics (8.694)

Journal of Controlled Release (7.164)

Current Opinion in Pharmacology (6.817)

Physiology:

Physiology (7.657)

Journal of Pineal Research (5.855)

Chronobiology International (5.576)

Journal of Mammary Gland Biology (5.446)

Journal of Physiology London (5.139)

Radiology, Nuclear Medicine & Medical Imaging:

Journal of Nuclear Medicine (7.022)

Radiology (6.066)

Neuroimage (5.932)

JACC-Cardiovascular Imaging (5.528)

Human Brain Mapping (5.107)

Virology:

PLoS Pathogens (9.079)

AIDS (6.348)

Retrovirology (5.236)

Journal of Virology (5.189)

Antiviral Research (4.439)

Zoology：

Wildlife Monographs（4.800）

Journal of Animal Ecology（4.457）

Journal of Comparative Neurology（3.774）

Developmental & Comparative Immunology（3.293）

Animal Behaviour（3.101）